A Bond with Birds

Featuring new paintings from Terance James Bond's 65th birthday exhibition

ARTISTS PROOF

Numbered limited edition: _____ of 1,000

THE WILDLIFE ART GALLERY 2011
IN PARTNERSHIP WITH ALAN MARSHALL AND MARION SCOTT

Text © Alan Marshall & Terance James Bond

Illustrations and photography
© Terance James Bond
Email: bond.art@btconnect.com

Publisher: Wildlife Art Gallery, 97 High Street,
Lavenham, Suffolk CO10 9PZ
Email: wildlifeartgallery@btinternet.com

Published in partnership with Alan Marshall
& Marion Scott

Design, layout and editing by Alan Marshall &
Marion Scott, Sutton, Norfolk
Email: scott_marshall@btinternet.com

Printed by Henry Ling, Dorchester
Email: enquiries@henryling.co.uk

A CIP record for this book is available from
the British Library.

ISBN: 978-0-9551695-0-2

Illustrated: front cover, *Barn Owl*; back cover, *Kingfisher*.
Title page, *Pied Wagtail*; opposite, *Little Owl*

Dedications

TJB. Anybody who earns their daily crust through
the process of selling a product simply cannot flourish
without one essential ingredient – customers!

To all those generous patrons who have made my
wonderful life possible over the last four decades, this
book is dedicated to you. THANK YOU!

ADMM. This book is dedicated to Betty Scott, who has
waited many years for the honour!

Contents

First impressions

Alan Marshall

This book has several goals. In no particular order, it is intended to delight, inform and educate. The first is easy: Terance James Bond paintings cannot fail to please bird-lovers and loyal followers alike. Terry's accompanying comments are always popular, providing a glimpse of his often irreverant character. His 'off-the-cuff' remarks also reveal his love and knowledge of the birds and trees he paints. Sometimes they can be serious and heartfelt. On other occasions, they can be downright frivolous. You never know what you will get when you ask Terry for some of his 'scribbles'!

As well as delighting readers, this book is intended to inform. For the first time in print, Terry has allowed someone to unveil his life story – or at least some edited highlights. For those already in possession of a 'TJB' picture, or those being tempted into ownership, you can now find out a great deal more about the man behind the bow tie. Having a TJB original is a pleasure and a privilege. The experience is even more enjoyable when you begin to understand where the passion for birds comes from, and why he is so determined to capture every last detail in his paintings.

Terry and his wife Jill have also allowed me to let readers into their home (albeit not literally). Sharing the star billing with the artist is a house and ten acres of land in rural Suffolk, which generates inspiration and perspiration in equal measure. From the very early days of his career as a bird painter, Terry has been determined to share any success with the subjects that provide his livelihood and have secured him his reputation. A considerable commitment in terms of time, effort and money has gone into the creation of a wildlife habitat designed to provide sanctuary for as many species as possible.

In terms of education, the intention of the book is to help readers understand better the species of birds painted by Terry, their habits, habitat, diet and conservation status. There is simply no room for complacency when it comes to Britain's wild birds. As in the sad case of the House and Tree Sparrows, once common species can become rarities seemingly overnight.

Even awareness of the plight of a species doesn't always help. The British Trust for Ornithology (BTO)'s data from the 2010 Garden BirdWatch show that the reporting rate for House Sparrows in UK gardens shows a continuing decline. Starling numbers are following a similar and equally worrying pattern.

Among farmland birds, where the rate of decline has been among the most alarming, there appears to have been a slowing in the fall in numbers. In *A Bond With Birds*, Terry refers often to the changes in farming practices since his childhood. Pressure on farms to produce food in greater volumes isn't conducive to habitat preservation. Yet, a balance must be achieved if many of the birds illustrated in these pages are to survive.

If you appreciate the pictures in this book, the chances are that you will love the birds themselves. Please therefore do everything you can to provide an environment and a food supply suitable for as many species as possible. You may not have Terry's ten acres of avian paradise, but every back garden is a potential nature reserve.

Data shown for bird species are provided by sources including the BTO and the Royal Society for the Protection of Birds (RSPB). Under Birds of Conservation Concern guidelines, birds are split into three categories of conservation importance: red, amber and green. Species on the red list are those that have shown a severe (at least 50 per cent) decline in UK breeding population over the past 25 years. Those on the amber list have suffered a moderate (25-49 per cent) decline, and birds on the green list are species that occur regularly in the UK. Statistics and conservation status were the most recent available at the time of writing.

Foreword
Andrew Haslen & Graham Barker

*Here at the Wildlife Art Gallery in Lavenham, we are proud
of our association with Terry, which stretches back to our first
exhibition in 1988. He may be just one of many artists to
have been showcased by us over the past 23 years, but his
distinctive style and enthusiastic following have made it
a particularly satisfying relationship for both parties.*

*Terry's passion for birds shines through in his paintings, but
the hidden side of TJB is his deep-seated commitment to
the countryside and its inhabitants that have provided him
with a living for more than 40 years. Like a good farmer
nurturing his land in order to produce the best meat
or crops, Terry ploughs time and money into his Suffolk
acreage in order that he (and we) can reap the rewards of
the wildlife on his doorstep.*

*We are lucky enough to represent many artists who devote
their lives to painting or sculpting wildlife. Their work
features numerous styles and involves a variety of media,
but all share a passion for animals and their environment.
In Terry's case, his almost fanatical attention to detail is
matched only by the tireless effort he and Jill devote to
their home and its surroundings.*

*While Terry's basic approach to painting birds has never
changed, with the emphasis always on faultless accuracy,
the scope of his work has expanded. To us, his most recent
pictures are the best he has ever produced. In this book,
readers will find some of his most ambitious paintings so far,
blending the natural beauty of trees with man-made objects
and, of course, birds in glorious technicolour.*

*We are delighted to act as publisher of Terry's fifth book,
which is also his first biography and presents the latest
portfolio of original images. We are also thrilled to be
exhibiting his new collection, which will cement his reputation
as Britain's best-loved bird artist.*

Painting for my life
Terance James Bond

My latest book is also my most personal, both in terms of the subject matter and in the way it has been produced. As a numbered, limited edition, it is designed to be exclusive and to appeal most to those who already know me and my work. After all, painting has been my life for more than 40 years, and it is time to share a little of that experience with others.

Virtually all of those involved in *A Bond With Birds* are friends, local professionals or both. Given that much of the written content focuses on my modest conservation efforts here in Suffolk, it seemed appropriate to have a 'home-grown' product.

Long-time supporter The Wildlife Art Gallery in Lavenham has acted as publisher, in association with clients, friends and editors Alan and Marion Marshall (née Scott). They are responsible for most of the words and all of the design, commuting occasionally from the Norfolk Broads during the long but relatively pain-free gestation period.

The book was printed in the UK, using partly wood-free paper. We could have saved money by printing in China, but it seemed inappropriate to focus on our conservation efforts here while shipping 1,000 books across 5,000 miles at considerable cost to the environment. I have probably left a big enough carbon footprint on this planet, without wishing to tread heavily at this late stage!

As ever, my long-suffering wife Jill helped provide ideas and inspiration, source images and bring back memories, all of which had to be collated in a form that could be used by the writers and designers. On top of all that, she was faced with catering challenges as meetings were convened inexplicably at Little Paddock around teatime.

On that subject, Little Paddock is one of the stars of this book. Not all of my pictures are set here, but the constant stream of feathered visitors to our patch of Suffolk paradise has a huge influence on my work. The Nuthatch pictured on page 65, for example, is making good use of one of the many Silver Birch trees outside my studio window.

From almost every vantage point we can see trees, water and so many birds. It doesn't matter if it is a visiting Pheasant

The artist at work in his Little Paddock studio

fleeing the gun, an opportunistic Kingfisher raiding the pond or our regular nesting Kestrels and Tawny Owls – there is always something to see. Bringing your subjects to your back garden has many advantages.

Painting has been my life's work, and I am very proud of the images hanging in people's homes, captured in books and printed on calendars. However, the money, time and effort spent on creating the perfect home and perfect habitat here in Suffolk is arguably a still greater achievement.

It is a major undertaking to manage a ten-acre natural landscape in such a way as to keep it attractive for wildlife and for the occupants of the modest bungalow in its midst. The expansion, development and management of the land is discussed in more detail later in the book, but Jill and I hope it represents a suitable recognition of our debt to the environment.

This book accompanies my first exhibition since 2006 (also staged by The Wildlife Art Gallery). That 'celebrated' my 60th birthday, while this one coincides with my 65th. Now that I am of pensionable age, I have to admit to some relief that I had the stamina to deliver a body of work sufficient to fill the gallery's walls and another book.

While many of the paintings contained herein are new and produced specifically for the show, I have indulged myself with a selection of work completed since the last exhibition. Retirement has been a dirty word in our household, and the studio has been manned regularly over the five years since *A Life In Detail*.

The paintings featured are some of the most challenging I have attempted. The faint-hearted may cringe at the Goshawk with his furry breakfast (page 104), but most of us hardened country dwellers will wish good riddance to a pesky grey squirrel. Jill and the gallery owners have pleaded with me to keep the body count low, so no more dead 'critters' will be found in these pages.

Big pictures, not always containing big birds, are a joy and a curse for an artist. The freedom to create on a large scale is wonderful. Then again, the sight of a large blank board on the easel can be intimidating, and the pain on the faces of would-be buyers when told the price is a heart-rending experience! Nonetheless, owls aplenty take up precious space in the book as they seem so often to need more tree than any other birds that I paint. The Little Owl (page 88) is particularly greedy for space, given his diminutive size.

I will admit to increasing selfishness as theoretical retirement looms. If I am to paint fewer pictures as the flesh becomes less willing, I want to concentrate on favourites or opportunities previously missed. The list of 'birds to paint' doesn't seem to get any shorter. Announcements such as "I want to do a Golden Eagle" are greeted with horror by Jill and gallery alike. They aren't quite brave enough to say that half-a-dozen Kingfishers would be easier to sell (and to paint).

As I said earlier, this is clearly a very personal book that I hope means as much to you as it does to me. It is aimed at bringing you closer to my world, providing a glimpse of what inspires my work and what creates my special 'bond with birds'.

Long Eared Owl
(Asio otus)

UK conservation status: green
Habitat: coniferous and
mixed woodland
Diet: small mammals (especially
voles) and some birds;
hunts at night

Smaller than a Wood Pigeon at 36cm from tufted crown to broad tail, the Long Eared Owl takes its name from the distinctive head feathers (not ears at all) that are raised when the owl is alarmed. Sporting mid-brown plumage with darker brown streaks, the bird boasts deep orange eyes. Northern birds migrate southwards, including owls from Continental Europe coming to winter in the UK, while southern birds are resident (forming a population of approximately 2,400 pairs). They usually perch close to the trunks of trees, generally in coniferous woods. They remain very still and aren't flushed easily from cover when approached.

TJB. "Many people associate owls with the hours of darkness: in reality, most are crepuscular by nature – active around sunset and sunrise. The Long Eared Owl is one of the truly nocturnal species, and generally goes about its business under cover of darkness. There are lots of trees in this painting. The intricate and complex shape of old pine trunks is a subject that appeals enormously: the colours and range of textures are certainly a challenge but, once you've got them right, the end result is very pleasing. While on the subject of trees, the Long Eared Owl exhibits another characteristic that is unique among our native species: it indulges in communal roosting during the winter months, with old willow and osier plantations the favoured sites."

Part One

Chapters

Paintings

Farmyard to schoolyard

It may surprise some readers to learn that Terance James Bond wasn't born with Winsor & Newton '97' coursing through his veins. While his distinctive style may suggest a direct line of descent from wildlife greats such as Archibald Thorburn or John James Audubon, there was no obvious painting pedigree. In fact, Terry put on his first 'show' in September 1946, exhibiting only those talents found typically in every newborn baby.

Growing up in post-war rural Britain meant few luxuries and a healthy appreciation of hard work and fresh air. Terry's eleven formative years spent on the Suffolk farm of his mother and stepfather exposed the young TJB to the wonders of nature in a landscape not yet corrupted by modern farming practices. As well as taking daily walks around the Assington farm with his stepfather and the dogs, his school holidays were generally spent labouring on the land. The occasional pheasant or pigeon would be shot for the pot, and Terry developed early driving skills at the wheel of the tractor.

There was little woodland on the farm itself but, fortunately for Terry, his stepfather's land was bordered on two sides by an old wood belonging to neighbours. It was here that he spent much of his time as a child, walking and watching birds. He therefore become a 'tree hugger' long before it was fashionable. Sadly, with many of the trees being Elm, it is unlikely that much of the original wood has survived.

Stanton's, the family business, was a traditional post-war arable farm, with no livestock to distract the young Terry. The animals he encountered on a daily basis were the farm's dogs, cats and some pet rabbits. The 200-acre Suffolk spread relied upon traditional farming and harvesting methods, resulting

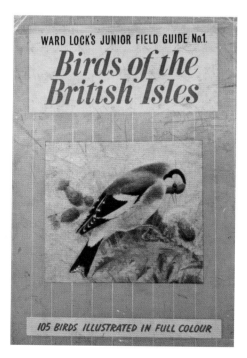

Above: portrait of the artist as a (very) young man; Below: the Brooke Bond prize

eventually in sacks of grain or potatoes stored in barns. This practice, in turn, attracted birds and the inevitable rats and mice. Animals tame and wild therefore become regular companions, while a healthy curiosity and a keen eye helped Terry learn quickly about the wildlife and environment around him. In spite of this, few people at that time could have guessed what direction his life would eventually take.

There were, however, some helpful clues along the way. Terry admits that he has drawn as long as he can remember. Any blank piece of paper was fair game and would eventually boast a TJB 'scribble'. In early schooldays, these were more likely to feature aeroplanes than birds.

In his final year at Bures County Primary Voluntary School, Terry was entered for and won a nationwide painting competition sponsored by tea supplier Brooke Bond. In recognition of his prolific and promising scribbles, he had, without prior knowledge, been chosen to represent his school. Given the entirely predictable subject chosen by the sponsor, namely 'The Tea Party', he promptly flouted convention and chose to use animals rather than people as his subjects. Even at the tender age of nine, he clearly had his priorities sorted.

While Terry on this occasion depicted aquatic life as the 'guests' at his party, the ten-shilling book token prize was invested wisely in a copy of *Birds of the British Isles*, which the Bonds still have in their library.

Published in 1957 by Ward, Lock & Co, the field guide was illustrated with paintings of British birds by Norfolk-born Frederick William Frohawk (1861-1946), one of the best ornithological artists of the period. Costing ten shillings and sixpence, the

Kestrel *(Falco tinnunculus)*

UK conservation status: amber
Habitat: open grassland, heath, farmland, towns
Diet: small mammals, young birds, insects and lizards or frogs
Also known as: Windhover

According to the poet Ted Hughes, the Kestrel's wings 'hold all creation in weightless quiet' (from *The Hawk in the Rain*). Most people's sightings are of birds 'hovering' over motorway verges, or perched patiently on telegraph wires alongside fields. Voles are the meal of choice, and just two or three a day are enough for an adult bird – which generally measures 34cm from head to tail. Kestrel numbers declined in the 1970s, reflecting changes in farming methods and resulting in their inclusion on the UK amber list. Recent figures suggest that the British population is now around 55,000 pairs. The name Kestrel is believed to derive from the French 'crécelle', meaning 'to rattle'. This is a reference to the bird's call.

TJB. "I offer no excuses for including several illustrations in this book of what has become my favourite bird of prey. The Kestrel was the first raptor that I became truly aware of during my early bird-watching days on my parents' farm in Suffolk. It will be familiar to anyone using Britain's motorways, and is easily recognisable as the only resident raptor that can hover in one spot while hunting for small mammals and large insects in the grass below. This unique behaviour has bestowed on the bird the apposite and charming country name of 'Windhover'. Surprisingly, there are still country dwellers who refer mistakenly to this bird as a Sparrowhawk. Apart from the obvious visual and behavioural difference, the Kestrel is actually a falcon and not a hawk."

book and its 105 colour plates clearly inspired the young TJB. He is to this day grateful for the early encouragement of form teacher Miss Noble in nurturing his budding talent.

More bird books were accumulated as Terry's interest grew. Painters such as Charles Tunnicliffe and Basil Ede impressed him with their attention to detail, although it was the work of the rather more obscure New Zealand artist Raymond Harris-Ching that was later to have the greatest impact.

Relatives were happy to encourage his healthy fascination with animals and birds. Aunt Peggy and Uncle Arthur in St Albans sent regular greetings cards illustrated by the likes of

Ede, while Terry remembers collecting Brooke Bond tea cards with their colourful Tunnicliffe bird images. A popular request at Christmas and birthdays was for additional bird books.

Given his unusual interests and the demands of a farming background, TJB fledged as an atypical teenager. Faced with a six-mile cycle ride to and from school in Bures, he shunned the football pitch and coffee bars frequented by his peers. Instead, he spent much of his leisure time on and around the farm, gaining valuable insights into the workings of the countryside and learning much about the local flora and fauna. Later in life, he would spend a great deal of time and money attempting to recreate the natural environment of his youth. 🖋

Nuthatch *(Sitta europaea)*

UK conservation status: green
Habitat: forest, woodland, towns
Diet: invertebrates, also hazelnuts, acorns, beechmast and seed;
feeds on tree trunk and branches, but also on the ground

The Nuthatch is similar in size to the Great Tit (around 14cm long), and resembles a small Woodpecker with its long, pointed black beak. It is usually seen inverted on a tree trunk, showing off a blue-grey back that is complemented by pale underbelly and chestnut to its sides and under its tail. The bird breeds mainly in central and southern England, as well as in Wales. It is a British resident, and birds seldom travel far from the woods in which they were born. There are believed to be just over 140,000 territories in the UK.

TJB. "Goodness knows how many Nuthatches I have painted during the past 40 years! One thing is certain: I will continue to illustrate this stunning little bird for as long as I can paint. Anyone who is familiar with my work will have come to the inevitable conclusion that I have an undiminished passion for trees. It is almost as though the arboreal association with this bird was designed with the artist in mind. The Nuthatch is linked inextricably to a woodland habitat and, as such, is one of the most acrobatic of our small resident birds. I generally illustrate the bird head down. Somehow it just seems right, and it helps no end with the general composition of the work. There is more than one Nuthatch painting in this book!"

House Martin

(Delichon urbicum)

UK conservation status: amber
Habitat: open country, towns
Diet: flying insects

House Martins originally nested on cliffs, but soon took to man-made structures, fixing their mud nest cups under the eaves. Each nest can take 10 days to build, and uses more than 1,000 beak-sized mud pellets. The UK breeding population is around 379,000 pairs. The 12cm-long birds have glossy blue-black upper parts and pure white undersides, distinctive white rumps and forked tails. They winter in Africa. Recent declines have earned them a place on the amber list.

TJB. "I can recall as a fledgling living with my grandparents while we were awaiting completion of a new bungalow on the farm. They ran a public house in Bures, renowned not only for the quality of the Trumans beer but for something entirely different. The building was rendered in a material that the local House Martin population found much to their liking. The whole under-eave frontage was festooned with their nests. One of my childhood memories is of lying in bed early on a summer morning and listening to the twittering of the birds. House Martin colonies can for some be a mixed blessing because of the accumulation of droppings and nesting mud on the walls and pavements below their nest sites. Perhaps in the early 1950s people were less fussy, as no one seemed to mind the guano. The habit of nesting in large colonies on the 'outside' of buildings helps identify the species from its close cousin, the Swallow, which nests inside buildings and is less communal in habit. One thing they do have in common is that their nests are built with mud interwoven with grass and straw. These birds are contemplating the muddy edges of a puddle – a typical scenario in the breeding season."

First sale to first show

While Terry's first efforts at painting were generally landscapes depicting life on the farm, there was a growing familiarity with the birds and beasts around him. This began increasingly to influence his artistic endeavours, at the same time as encouragement and guidance were helping him raise the standard of his pictures. Even at such an early age, he paid close attention to detail and tended to reproduce his subjects life size. Fortunately, most Suffolk wildlife generally comes in small packages...

Encouraged by his latest art teacher Mary Chamberlain at the new secondary modern school in nearby Stoke-by-Nayland, Terry concentrated on improving his work, with the result that his first commercial sale was achieved at the age of just 13. A watercolour of Pheasants at roost went to a neighbouring farmer for seven shillings and sixpence.

To put this in perspective, Terry's weekly pocket money at the time was just two shillings and sixpence. A career in wildlife art had already begun, even though it would take another decade before it became his livelihood. In the meantime, school friends were also to become customers, as Terry augmented his income with private sales. The attitude of his teachers to such precocious behaviour hasn't been reported!

Such minor transactions aside, a more orthodox use of his skills with a pencil was initially on the agenda. Leaving school with a clutch of GCE passes (including the inevitable credit in Art & Craft), and having attained the status of head prefect, he headed into the world of engineering. The received wisdom was that a career as a technical illustrator was his destiny, perhaps with the occasional bird painting on the side.

As is so often the way, things didn't go quite to plan. Having joined Whitlock Brothers of Great Yeldham (near the Essex town of Halstead) with a view to producing highly detailed drawings of the firm's earthmoving equipment (including the famous Dinkum Diggers), Terry was faced with a complete culture shock.

He found himself assigned to the company's production line and given other manual tasks aimed at providing him with a thorough understanding of the processes involved in making these machines. While the adult Terry was eventually to become a great fan of such mechanical marvels, the teenager became rapidly disillusioned with this alien and talent-stifling environment. TJB therefore began to look elsewhere for a comfortable seat at a drawing board.

While searching for more suitable full-time employment, he worked at a local fruit farm in Assington, which was close to the family farm and the public house run by his grandparents. This fairly enjoyable interlude reawakened his interest in the great outdoors, particularly the birds and trees. One species that made a strong impression was the much maligned Bullfinch (see page 59), hated by fruit farmers but beloved of bird artists.

Terry was now living in Assington with his grandparents, after his mother, stepfather and sister had emigrated to Australia. He soon found a new position in a drawing office (at Esso Petroleum subsidiary APL Heating). Working in Ipswich with a tee square on plans for central heating systems may have been a step in the right direction, but it hardly provided the artistic freedom for which the budding painter yearned. Still, the job was to result in an encounter with the future Mrs Bond, who was to play a key role in Terry's later and most significant change in direction.

While visiting a friend who worked at APL, the delectable Jill Wright caught Terry's eye, and romantic assignations soon followed. From the outset, Jill demonstrated remarkable tolerance and enthusiasm, both valuable attributes when it comes to sharing life with an artist.

Not for them evenings in the pub or Saturday afternoons at the football stadium. The TJB courtship involved long, often cold and damp, walks in the countryside. Perhaps being around her father's fresh fish shop in Ipswich had helped acclimatise Jill! This new stability in Terry's personal life was reflected on the employment front, with a new job at Hadleigh-based storage vessel supplier Cookson & Zinn.

In his spare time, he continued to swap tee square for paintbrush, and in 1969 he placed three small paintings of British mammals in a local art exhibition. The far-sighted and altruistic Jack Haste had entered Terry's life, and was to help push forward his artistic ambitions.

The show in question was staged annually by Mr Haste at his Ipswich gallery, and aimed to encourage non-professional artists to exhibit their work for the first time. Terry retains a vivid memory of nervously entering the gallery with Jill on a Saturday morning. His three paintings (Hedgehog, Stoat and Red Squirrel) hung proudly with the other exhibition entries, but they had seemingly been defiled by the addition of red spots. Asking for the offending dots to be removed, the young artist was informed politely that they signified a sale! His first 'show' was a sell-out, with the pictures realising five pounds apiece – dwarfing his wages of three pounds and ten shillings a week.

Terry also remembers submitting a watercolour of five Shelduck against a backdrop of trees in the mist – perhaps his first 'professional' attempt at marrying birds and landscape. His recollection is that his then employer, Mr Cookson, acquired the painting. Inspired by this success and backed by the generosity and encouragement of Mr Haste, Terry asked about the possibility of staging a small exhibition of his own. Given the gallery owner's blessing and in receipt of a request for 15-20 pictures, he got painting. As Terry explains, it is almost impossible to convey the feeling of excitement and gratitude that resulted from his initial sales.

There is no doubt that Jack Haste helped fan the flames of Terry's desire to become a professional wildlife artist. Over a period of around 18 years, the Haste Gallery played host to five or six TJB exhibitions and accounted for more than a hundred picture sales.

The big day and big decisions

Equally exciting and life-changing was Terry's forthcoming marriage to Jill. In May 1970, they wed at St Augustine's church in Ipswich, with a very modest reception in the town's Golden Hind pub. Deciding to spend their lives together was an easy decision for a couple who had, in their own words, "dovetailed" so neatly, but there would be plenty of challenges ahead.

Both Terry and Jill were near the beginning of their careers, so hardly flush with cash. They needed somewhere to live, but they couldn't afford to aim too high. Although in those days you could buy a three-bedroom detached bungalow in Suffolk for £5,000, neither of them had such a sum. A meeting with the local building society procured an alarming mortgage which, with a painfully accumulated deposit of £300, gave them a budget of £4,000.

Suffolk's charming towns and villages were clearly out of the question but, by heading north of the East Anglian border, a suitable (and affordable) home was found at New Buckenham in the Brecklands region of Norfolk. In an early but typical display of 'Bondian' determination, the couple had married, found a three-bedroom chalet bungalow and both changed jobs in the space of five weeks – with Terry joining the drawing office of Haden Young of Norwich. He now had more space to paint in comfort (using a spare bedroom), with the upcoming exhibition at the Haste Gallery providing fresh impetus to get stuck in.

May 1971 was to be a turning point on the road to artistic fame and (relative) fortune. It saw TJB stage his first one-man show of bird paintings in Ipswich. The Haste Gallery arranged a private view, with the result that each of the 25 pictures sold immediately and all parties celebrated the welcome but unexpected success. So pleased was Mr Haste that a follow-up show was requested, to take place just over a year later.

Before the second exhibition in the summer of 1972, the Bonds' fortunes had improved, so they turned their backs on Norfolk and migrated back south to the familiar surroundings of Suffolk's Babergh district. Terry was now engaged in engineering design with Cooksons – the same company that had employed him before the move north. However, he found himself faced with a major decision. Should he take the safe option and remain in full-time employment, or should he gamble on a perilous career as a professional artist?

At this point, Terry's future as a bird painter hung in the balance. If he had remained a part-time 'hobby' painter, most of us would never have seen the impressive avian portraits that were to flow from his brushes. Books such as this would certainly never have seen the light of day.

Fortunately, Mrs Bond took matters into her own hands, committing herself to many more years as a 'wage slave' so that he could swap the drawing board for an easel. She had an absolute belief in Terry's ability, confident that his paintings would continue to sell – and in greater numbers and for higher prices. While her confidence was ultimately rewarded, it must have been a nerve-wracking time for the Bonds.

Terry has always been quick to acknowledge his wife's role in developing his career. "Jill is the most perceptive and intelligent wife I could have been blessed with," he says. "She could see that I had a talent that needed to be encouraged, and one that would develop given the opportunity." He argues persuasively that he owes his success to her support and confidence in his abilities.

Perhaps as a reward for her brave decision, Jill went on to forge her own successful career in engineering, eventually becoming a director of a local business – before setting that aside to manage Terry's life, their home and his business affairs.

Stonechat
(Saxicola torquatus)

UK conservation status: green
Habitat: open country, scrub
**Diet: invertebrates and occasional
seeds or berries; hunts from perch,
picking up food from the ground**

Stonechats are attractive, Robin-sized birds
of around 12cm that breed in western and
southern parts of Britain, but will spread more
widely during the winter months. The male
bird has a striking black head, accompanied by
white around the side of the neck. He sports
an orange-red waistcoat and a brown jacket.
The female bird has less orange on her breast
and doesn't wear the black cap. The Stonechat's
name is derived from a call that resembles two
stones being tapped together. It can be spotted
by the habit of wing-flicking while perched on
low bushes or posts. The UK population is
estimated at 15,000 pairs.

TJB. "The seaward perimeter of the RSPB
Reserve at Minsmere on the Suffolk coast
presents the walker with one of the more
unusual features of this part of the heathland –
large numbers of huge concrete blocks. These
are remnants of military defences deployed
during World War II and, presumably, were built
along the edge of the beach to prevent the
landing of enemy tanks. As far as the resident
population of Stonechats is concerned, they
were put there for their benefit. Presumably,
these lumps of masonry absorb a lot of heat
on a sunny day, so perhaps they offer the birds
the double benefit of an observation post and
a large foot warmer... The sight of Stonechats
in full breeding plumage is a wonderful thing,
and they also look fantastic sitting on the
surrounding gorse bushes, with the yellow
flowers adding contrast to their striking
plumage. I have to say I find the gorse bushes
more inspiring from an artistic point of view
than the aforementioned concrete blocks!"

Part Two

Chapters

Paintings

A brush with royalty

I t is easy to underestimate the sheer enormity of the risk involved in the Bonds' decision to allow Terry to 'turn professional'. It is one thing to sell out two local exhibitions as a young artist when there is a full-time job to subsidise the hobby. It is quite another to swap a regular income for the uncertainty of artistic endeavour. The couple decided to give it two years. Jill would remain at work, and if things didn't go to plan Terry would resume his career in engineering.

However, the timely arrival of Terry's first private commissions helped bolster his confidence and improved greatly the prospects of success. Art-lovers who attended the early exhibitions in Ipswich began to enquire through the Haste Gallery if TJB would paint for them. Word spread fast and if the Bonds had owned a telephone it would have been ringing off the hook.

Such was Terry's belief in the quality of his work that, in 1977, he targeted a particularly high-profile 'customer'. As the British public was celebrating Her Majesty The Queen's silver jubilee, TJB thought the patron of the Royal Society for the Protection of Birds (RSPB) might like to have one of his paintings hanging in one of her several homes.

While the motive was largely to please The Queen and hopefully earn at least an acknowledgement, the Bonds appreciated that any resulting publicity could do no harm. Not surprisingly, the local press got wind of the story and Terry's own profile benefited from the exposure. Before heading to its more prestigious home, the painting of two Tawny Owls was hung in the Haste Gallery, bedecked with a red, white and blue sash.

Terry and Jill accompanied the owls to the royal estate at Sandringham, but there was no audience with The Queen. However, they were given a tour of the house and its picture gallery by The Queen's equerry. A letter of thanks from HRH arrived in the following day's post. Not exactly 'By Royal Appointment', but at least a brush with royalty.

Some people say that it is bad luck to have images of owls in the home. On this occasion, it doesn't appear to have turned out too badly for the Bonds or HRH...

Above: Terry with the painting destined for Her Majesty The Queen

'Winter Diners' (overleaf)

TJB. "The feeding of garden birds during the winter is now a widespread and popular pastime for many wildlife lovers, and the manufacture and supply of proprietary bird food has become a multi-million-pound industry. Simply chucking some stale bread or scraps into the garden is no longer enough. Not only is the nutritional content low, but you may attract more rats than Robins. A bewildering variety of seed types and specially formulated mixes is now available, matched only by an equally impressive range of feeding devices. At least 20 different species visit my own feeding stations at various times during the coldest weather, and all of the birds illustrated here have at one time or another graced my feeders. Usually I resist representing more than one species in a painting, but the client who commissioned this particular work expressed a wish for all of his regular 'customers' to be included in the composition. However, the species list that he presented was extremely comprehensive, so for the sake of artistic integrity I restricted myself to the more common of our *Winter Diners*."

Merlin *(Falco columbarius)*

UK conservation status: amber
Habitat: moorland, heath,
open coniferous forest
Diet: mostly small birds caught by pursuit
low over open ground
Also known as: Stone Falcon

Once very popular for falconry, particularly with women, the pint-sized (28cm) Merlin was used to chase down Skylarks over heath and moorland. Numbers rise in the winter thanks to the arrival of breeding Icelandic birds. In spite of a recovering British population since the 1980s (when we were down to just 550 pairs), the bird remains on the UK amber list, with loss of moorland habitat a threat. Recent data suggest there are just 1,300 British pairs. Merlins leave their upland breeding grounds between August and October, returning in April and May. During the winter months, they are often sighted near coasts, and inland in low-lying areas.

TJB. "This is our smallest British falcon, only slightly bigger than a Mistle Thrush. The painting here depicts a mature male, and what a super chap he is. I generally paint the cock bird of any raptor, simply because they are usually the most striking in appearance, if not necessarily the biggest. The rules are clearly different in ornithology! The Merlin is a bird of open moorland and upland environments, and it specialises in the aerial hunting of prey such as Meadow Pipits, Skylarks and Wheatears. These are taken usually after a low-level, high-speed pursuit. The Merlin will lock on to its quarry and follow every twist and turn of the intended victim; unless the target is smart or lucky (or both), the end result is inevitable."

A date for the calendar

By 1980, Terry had been painting professionally for around eight years and was building steadily a reputation for his detailed portrayals of British birds. In 1981, he was invited to submit work for an exhibition staged by the RSPB in London on the permanently moored ship 'Tattershall Castle' which, in those days, acted as a floating gallery on the River Thames. Terry's recollection is that he was the only artist to sell a painting, causing a visiting Jill great excitement, even though this wasn't to be the most significant aspect of the show.

Standing behind Terry during the exhibition's private viewing was an individual who would help further the artist's career. Brian Rushton was the Design & Product Manager for the UK's leading advertising publisher, and was clearly impressed by Terry's work. This led to a phone call and a subsequent meeting at which the use of TJB paintings on fine art business calendars was discussed.

Bemrose of Derby agreed terms with Terry, introducing his images to the popular annual publication and beginning an association that continued for almost 30 years. During this time, Terry has produced more than 250 paintings for large-format fine art calendars plus at least 80 small images for slimline versions.

The arrangement led to a number of benefits, including a new source of income, greater exposure and, through a connection between the publishers and the RSPB, a relationship with the country's foremost bird conservation body that has lasted until the present day.

In Terry's opinion, this was to be the turning point in his artistic career. The Bemrose relationship demonstrated that he didn't have to rely totally on unpredictable commissions or occasional exhibitions. It also further convinced him of the quality and increasing desirability of his work. 🖋

Kingfisher *(Alcedo atthis)*

**UK conservation status: amber
Habitat: rivers, marshes, lakes, coast
Diet: mostly freshwater fish, also
aquatic invertebrates. Hunts from
perch or by hovering prior to dive
Also known as: Halcyon**

Unmistakable, but still hard to spot, the Kingfisher
is generally seen as a jewel-like blur flashing
along the river bank. Those lucky enough to see
a stationary bird (just 16cm in height) can hardly
believe the colours, the length of the beak and the
size of fish waiting to be consumed or delivered
to young. A full brood of chicks can consume
more than 100 fish a day. Already a short-lived
bird, harsh winters can reduce dramatically
Kingfisher numbers, as ice prevents them from
feeding. This means they often take winter breaks
on the coast, where fishing is easier. In the UK,
there are approximately 57,000 pairs.

*It was the rainbow gave thee birth,
And left thee all her lovely hues*
(William Henry Davies: *The Kingfisher*)

TJB. "We are back on the east coast here, and the
magnetic appeal of old boats and their associated
paraphernalia again proved irresistible. This is one of
my favourite paintings. The colour range throughout
the work is kept to a minimum, with the peeling
paint and ropes reflecting some of the underlying
plumage colours of the subject. The photographic
equipment I use is of the large and professional
type and, as such, can sometimes attract attention
from passers-by. On one occasion, when I was
photographing old mooring ropes, I drew the
attention of the boat owner, who was intrigued
as to why I should want to photograph just this
slightly scruffy portion of the old vessel. Having
explained in some detail exactly what I was doing
and why, the owner immediately responded by
saying, 'Cor blast, old mate, you doont want ter
paint that old roop, I'll git you a new bit'. It took
some explaining to convince him that this 'old bita
roop' was just what I wanted."

Atlantic crossing

Readers should now be very familiar with Terry's meticulous paintings of indigenous British bird species, but a few of the sharp-eyed among you may have noted in earlier books the occasional alien intruder such as Blue Jays or American Kestrels. Had certain transatlantic career opportunities been followed up, Terry's bond could have been with North American birds.

Early exposure to the large and potentially lucrative US art market was gained in 1974, when TJB was given the chance to hold an exhibition in a gallery just off New York's glamorous Fifth Avenue. Jill was at that time working for a US-owned company, and when its president was in the UK he saw some of Terry's work and set the wheels in motion for what was to be another sell-out show.

More than a decade later, the publication of TJB's first book resulted in another North American dalliance. Terry was in 1987 approached by a publishing agent with contacts among several book publishers. He committed to producing the 96-page *Birds: the Paintings of Terance James Bond*, which was launched in 1988 by Lutterworth Press of Cambridge (with a subsequent limited-edition, leather-bound version). At the same time, through the same agent, he was introduced to a fine art print publisher in Florida by the name of Mill Pond Press.

It was a very exciting time, as not every British wildlife painter is offered the chance to forge a relationship with what was then considered to be the leading US fine art publisher of natural history subjects. No doubt the money would have been equally impressive, but there were rather more doubts over the changes in lifestyle and the type of work to be undertaken.

Sticking with British species was apparently a non-starter as far as North American publishers were concerned. The perceived level of interest among Americans in UK species was low. Also, they couldn't understand why someone would want to paint a Sparrow when there were Cardinals about!

Even Terry's specialisation in birds would have been at risk, as the US wildlife art market at that time apparently demanded majestic American mammals and dramatic landscapes. A half-hearted effort was made by Terry to get the publisher interested in North American birds of prey, but to no avail.

American Kestrel from TJB's first book published in 1988

During the three-year association, and two largely enjoyable visits to Florida, Terry got to rub shoulders with renowned international wildlife artists such as Sir Peter Scott, Roger Tory Petersen, Robert Bateman and Carl Brenders. Seeing his work judged and displayed alongside that of such illustrious peers provided a confidence boost, and one that helped him reach the difficult decision to plough his own furrow back in the UK.

He had realised that British birds remained his first love – and his natural environment was the rolling Suffolk countryside. There was to be no permanent Atlantic crossing. To this day, there are no regrets at having stuck close to his roots. 🐦

Robin *(Erithacus rubecula)*

UK conservation status: green
Habitat: forest, woodland, towns, gardens
Diet: insects, larvae; fruit and seeds in winter
Also known as: Redbreast

While surprisingly aggressive towards intruders, the Robin's popular image is one of a cheeky familiarity. Male and female (around 14cm in height) look the same, but youngsters sport spotted waistcoats. The song is a delight, and the Robin is one of the few British birds that sings year round. As with the Nightingale, the song is usually delivered from a bush or tree. Robins are often active when few other birds are about – up early for the dawn chorus and still singing as darkness falls. In common with other songbirds, Robins can be short-lived. Many succumb to cold, starvation and disease, in spite of the warm welcome afforded them in the British garden. Robins in the UK occupy about 5.5 million territories.

TJB. "What is there to say about this familiar bird, beloved by everyone? The species is associated inextricably with the festive season, and the image of the Robin is vital to the Christmas card trade. During the winter, many resident birds migrate to the near Continent. In the breeding season, the Robin is highly territorial and will fight to the death (sometimes literally) in defence of its own patch. Voted Britain's national bird 50 years ago, the Robin retains a very special place in our hearts. Has it occurred to you that this is one of very few resident birds bearing a human name? Strictly speaking, this is a woodland bird that has adapted to, and become integrated with, urban life. While I have painted the Robin in both natural and urban environments, the client who commissioned this particular image asked for a definite garden setting. The flowerpots harmonise well with the colours of the bird, and were the obvious choice."

Part Three

Chapters

Paintings

The Lavenham connection

Fans of TJB's work over the past couple of decades will be aware of the involvement of the Wildlife Art Gallery in Lavenham, which was the first specialised showcase for bird and animal painters. The gallery acts as publisher for this book, and will be exhibiting the latest TJB work in September 2011 as Terry reaches 65 years of age. It was also responsible for his last show in September 2006, which saw the launch of Terry's previous book *A Life in Detail*.

The Suffolk gallery established in 1988 by Andrew Haslen and Graham Barker effectively took over the TJB mantle from the Haste Gallery with which Terry had been associated between 1970 and the late 1980s. With retirement beckoning for Jack Haste, Terry hooked up with the new Lavenham gallery in the beautifully preserved Suffolk village just a few miles from his home.

In fact, Terry and Jill had crossed paths with Andrew in the mid-1980s when he was staging wildlife art exhibitions at different venues in Suffolk. He would hire village halls or other people's galleries for the shows, and Terry's work had occasionally featured.

The Wildlife Art Gallery's inaugural exhibition in 1988 featured Terry's work, and his paintings have brightened the gallery's walls on many occasions in the intervening years. Andrew and Graham have since relocated in the medieval wool town, moving close to the famous Swan Hotel in the heart of the village. Terry has made the short journey with them. It has been a symbiotic relationship, with Terry's enthusiastic followers helping ensure the sale of many paintings while the artist has benefited from the gallery's specialisation and growing reputation.

During the late 1980s, Jill had been considering the possibility of 'retiring' early from her full-time job and staying at home to look after the artist, their dogs (they owned five Labradors over a 25-year period) and the expanding wildlife haven being created around their home. Over the previous decade, the Bonds had been adding to the acreage surrounding their bungalow near Kersey (see Part Four), with the aim of attracting bird species to a well-managed natural habitat.

Since 1990, Jill has managed successfully the TJB business empire, while typing manuscripts, keeping the accounts in order and generally clearing the way for Terry's uninterrupted use of the brush and easel. She has played a vital role in developing the landscape around their home and, given the necessary commitment to this major undertaking, her decision proved well timed.

Outside the Wildlife Art Gallery in Lavenham, June 2011. From left to right: Terance James Bond, Andrew Haslen and Graham Barker. (Photograph: Alan Marshall)

Kestrel

TJB. "Those who are familiar with my paintings know that I have a passion for rendering considerable detail and content in a picture, and this often results in a large and comprehensive work. This practice stems from my obsessive desire to illustrate everything just as I see it, and to give equal importance to the subject's habitat. Without doubt, I get as much pleasure from illustrating the accompanying details of a composition, such as logs, stones and tree trunks, all of which display an irresistible combination of light and shade. This helps delineate their textures and surfaces. Once in a while, I feel the need to complete a particular work over a shorter period and believe that the bird is all that is required to complete the piece. This portrait of a male Kestrel is just such a painting. It reveals enough of the habitat to hint at the bird's location, but the main focus is the subject itself. Some of my collectors admit freely that they prefer this type of painting and, as a result, I usually complete one or two such studies during the course of a working year."

Nightingale *(Luscinia megarhynchos)*

UK conservation status: amber
Habitat: thickets, woodland
Diet: insects, particularly beetles and ants; plus berries in autumn
Also known as: Barley Bird

The collective noun for the Nightingale is 'Watch'. This, sadly, is very hard to do as these small brown birds (16cm in length) have always been hard to spot. Dwindling numbers now make this even more difficult – the British population is down to just 7,500 males. The Nightingale is most unlikely ever to have sung in Berkeley Square, unless it was much more heavily wooded in the past! While the bird can only be described as rather plain, its song makes up for the lack of visual glamour, featuring a rapid succession of high, low and rich notes unrivalled among British birds. Sadly, even an 'X Factor' voice doesn't get this singer noticed. It breeds mostly south of the Severn-Wash line and east from Dorset to Kent. The highest densities are found in Essex, Suffolk, Norfolk, Kent and Sussex. The Nightingale arrives in April and sings until early June, leaving between July and September.

O Nightingale that on yon bloomy spray,
Warbl'st at eve, when all the Woods are still
Thou with fresh hope the lover's heart dost fill,
While the jolly hours lead on propitious May,
Thy liquid notes that close the eye of day,
First heard before the shallow Cuckoo's bill...
(John Milton: *To The Nightingale*)

TJB. "Not so many years ago, Nightingales would sing in our garden. Sadly, they no longer visit. Something odd is happening to the fortunes of the Nightingale. In complete contrast to the gradual northwards movement of many other examples of flora and fauna, the Nightingale seems to be retreating back to the south coast. The species was never widespread, and the bird was always more common south of the Thames. Strangely enough, another summer visitor, the Cuckoo, is also undergoing a reduction in range. Famed for its incredible song, the Nightingale is vocal for only a few weeks of the early summer. May is the month for the Nightingale's song; and, despite its name, the bird does sing during the day. Several well-meaning people have informed me that they have heard the Nightingale's song but, on closer examination, it turns out that the locality and the season make this unlikely. People often confuse the melodious trilling of a Robin or Song Thrush with the far richer variety of the Nightingale, as both of these rival performers will sing after dark. The Nightingale's wonderful repertoire is delivered usually from deep cover as it favours deciduous woodland with generous understory. I have lost count of the occasions on which I have stood only a few yards from the bird, entranced by its song, but completely unable to pinpoint its source."

A style of his own

Terance James Bond – Live in Studio One!

From the outset, Terry failed to conform to the stereotype of the wildlife artist. Admittedly, the early landscape watercolours produced during his schooldays may have been less remarkable than his later work, but he still demonstrated an unusual eye for detail. Not for him the 'unfinished' style of painting where impressions are given of key features. For Terry, a tractor cannot be a loosely defined red shape in a field, but has to be recognisable down to the manufacturer's badge and the driver's hairstyle!

Not everyone appreciates such great attention to detail. His art tutors were often dismayed at his insistence on keeping painting long after they thought the picture was complete. At Stoke-by-Nayland secondary modern, Mary Chamberlain told him he was the best student she'd ever had – but that she hated everything he painted!

Terry, however, stuck to his guns. As birds became his specialisation, he became still more committed to capturing every detail. Depicting his subjects full size is a reflection of that desire for ultimate accuracy. A close encounter with the work of Raymond Harris-Ching provided an additional incentive, so impressed was young Terry by the New Zealand painter's work.

In the 1960s, Ching began to exhibit and sell paintings of birds, thus making him a contemporary of TJB. A major sell-out exhibition in Auckland, which showcased his highly detailed watercolours created using a dry brush technique, brought him to the attention of Sir William Collins of Collins Publishers. On moving to London, where he rubbed shoulders

Tawny Owl *(Strix aluco)*

UK conservation status: green
Habitat: forest, woodland, towns
Diet: small mammals, birds, amphibians,
worms and beetles; hunts mostly between
dusk and dawn
Also known as: Brown Owl

Sweet Suffolk Owl, so trimly dight
With feathers like a lady bright,
Thou sing'st alone, sitting by night,
Te whit, te whoo! Te whit, te whoo!
The note, that forth so freely rolls,
With shrill command the mouse controls,
And sings a dirge for dying souls,
Te whit, te whoo! Te whit, te whoo!
(Anonymous: Sweet Suffolk Owl)

The Tawny Owl is about the size of a Pigeon, standing some 38cm tall. It has a rounded body and head, with a ring of dark feathers around its face. The bird is largely reddish brown above, hence the alternative name 'Brown Owl'. It has paler undersides. The Tawny Owl is a widespread breeding species in England, Wales and Scotland, but the Irish never get to hear its familiar call. The UK population is put at around 19,000 pairs. Given its nocturnal nature, you are more likely to hear than see the bird, although regurgitated pellets beneath a roosting spot may give away its location on a branch close to the tree trunk. Birds are mainly resident, and established pairs probably never leave their territories. Young birds disperse from their breeding grounds in the autumn. The 'te whit, te whoo' call appears in Shakespeare's *Love's Labour's Lost* In fact, the male bird hoots (te whoo) and the female responds (te whit).

TJB. "The Tawny is about as 'owly' as it gets. If a committee was convened and asked to sit down and design the 'standard' owl, this is what the end result would look like. I have probably painted more 'Tawnies' than any other owl during my career as a bird artist, but it still remains my personal preference from the six species on the British List. Again, I suspect that it is the association of woodland that makes this owl a preferred subject. Having made the decision to paint yet another tree-biased work, this particular image was really more a portrait of the bird. The 'Sweet Suffolk Owl' features elsewhere in this publication as the subject of a very large set piece."

with naturalist and artist Sir Peter Scott, Ching was introduced to The Reader's Digest which, with Collins, had been planning a major book on the birds of Britain. The ambitious volume, in addition to containing all the accurate information on British birds, was to have enough style and drama to appeal to those not normally attracted by field guides. Ching became the principal artist for *The Reader's Digest Book of British Birds*, which required 230 full-colour portraits – all of which were delivered within a year, at great cost to the artist's health.

Published in 1969, the title became the world's biggest-selling bird book, translated into more than ten European languages. Terry, like so many others, saw it as the bird lover's bible.

Terry encountered Ching's work at a London exhibition, which he visited as a young man with Jill on his arm. One painting, of a Kestrel on a sack of straw, captured his imagination. Every stitch was visible on the sack, as was each individual straw and, of course, the bird's glorious feathers. To Terry, it was a challenge to match (or, better still, surpass) that level of detail and that quality of work.

The die was cast. While most other bird painters would spend time in the field with their sketchbooks or even their easels and paints, Terry would produce his work exclusively in a studio environment. He would, and still does, produce rough drawings to set out his ideas. However, thanks to a remarkable memory and the draughtsman's eye, he can reproduce sights seen in the field without the help of endless sketchbooks.

The other love of Terry's artistic life has also played a role. He admits that, if painting hadn't worked out, he would probably have been a professional photographer. From Jill's wedding present of a 35mm Pentax in 1970, he has become addicted to using the best available equipment. His use of medium-format Hasselblad cameras, first film and now digital, has enabled him to capture magical images – some of which may be used indirectly in his most challenging paintings.

Starting with inexpensive watercolours at school, Terry had moved quickly to using gouache, a more opaque version of watercolour. After some unsuccessful early experiments with oils, where the slow-drying properties clashed with his painting style, he stuck with gouache throughout the 1970s and 1980s, producing hundreds of strong, vivid paintings.

While talking with American publishers in the late 1980s, he was introduced to US acrylic paints. These were to have a profound effect on his work. Being more transparent than gouache, the change meant much more brush work to build up

layers of colour. However, few would disagree that his colours brightened and textures deepened using the new medium. Quick drying, permanent and easy to work with, acrylics have provided the richness of oils without the drawbacks.

Terry explains that all of the paintings start with detailed drawings on boards that he hand-coats himself with gesso. Originally a white paint mixture using a combination of chalk or gypsum, this is more often nowadays based on an acrylic polymer medium. It is used to prime surfaces such as canvas or artist's boards so as to allow the paint to be absorbed and adhere more readily. Virtually everything that is to appear in Terry's finished painting will be drawn painstakingly in pencil on to the prepared board. All he then has to do is colour it in!

In fact, once satisfied with the pencil drawing, Terry proceeds to 'line out' the work with black paint, using a fine sable brush

(see image below left). This both seals the image and fixes in place the original pencil lines. It also allows the drawing to be seen through the various layers of under-painting.

From here, Terry will begin to apply several opaque coats, creating an approximation of the desired finish colour. He will be seeking to create an impression of the texture of the background matter, be it grass, tree bark or water.

The next stage sees the building up of the detail, which is the most time-consuming part of the process as thousands of brush strokes are required, using very fine sable brushes that Terry consumes in huge numbers. Once an area has been detailed, there may be another coat of transparent colour.

Perhaps uniquely, the TJB approach is to save the principal subject to last – the bird. He sees this as a treat after weeks of crafting a background of twigs and branches, or bark and barbed wire. Terry always begins his birds at the tail, and works up to the head. The eye is often the last thing to be painted.

Reflecting his own appreciation of the natural environment, his work will often put great emphasis on trees, lichen-encrusted rocks, field stubble and water in many forms. When in an indulgent mood, and seeking a break from commissions of garden favourites, he will take on a bigger challenge – which is not necessarily a bigger bird. Some of his most successful works actually feature small birds against large and complex backgrounds (see Little Owl in a lime tree on pages 88 and 89).

From early vignettes to recent major works and even the latest 'tinies' seen within the pages of this book, TJB has succeeded in delivering a large and varied body of work that undoubtedly has improved with age.

There has always been a musical backdrop to Terry's life. He has memories from his secondary school days of evening maths tuition when approaching his GCEs. The teacher and his wife would play classical music after the lessons had ended. The pieces would be replayed in Terry's head as he cycled home, resulting in a lasting passion.

BBC Radio 3 plays during his working day, and Terry can associate specific paintings with particular passages, and vice versa. Sometimes he gets so caught up in the music that the painting grinds to a halt. On other occasions, he can benefit from a fresh surge of inspiration as the notes echo around the studio.

His major works must sometimes seem like concertos and symphonies, both in terms of the composition time and their complexity. Perhaps the smaller paintings are more akin to shorter movements or operatic arias, quicker to create but no less satisfying.

Left: adding large areas of water to the land at Little Paddock has attracted many more subjects for Terry's paintings

Opposite: a preparatory study for the Nuthatch painting that appears on page 85 – all of the paintings start with detailed drawings on boards that he hand-coats himself with gesso

A higher profile

From china plates to Christmas cards, TJB's paintings have made plenty of appearances outside of art galleries. Commissions are a blessing and a curse in equal measure, as they provide valuable income, but limit an artist's freedom to paint what he likes, when he likes. Terry is no exception, accepting most requests with gratitude, but at all times dreaming of a free choice of subject, size and timing. He will try and negotiate some room for manoeuvre when discussing the commission, or even persuade the client to change his or her mind if the initial idea doesn't appeal.

It was the early exhibitions that got his professional career off the ground, but a steady stream of commissions that kept Terry airborne. The regular work provided by the annual calendar commitment then became another critical element of early success, with the contract also providing valuable exposure.

Terry argues that his most significant publishing breakthrough was the opportunity to supply artwork for fine art business calendars. He points out that the Bemrose Group, which published the calendars, became an integral part of his career from 1980 onwards.

During this 30-year period, somewhere in the region of 70 calendars of various types have been published in association with organisations such as the RSPB, National Westminster Bank, Guardian Direct, Glaxo, wildlife societies, pet food manufacturers, Wedgwood, Danbury Mint and many others.

The large-format 'British Birds' calendar was almost the perfect medium to show off Terry's increasingly complex paintings, where background detail rivals that of the bird's plumage in terms of painstaking brushwork. Equally popular were the slimline RSPB calendars which, although not the ideal showcase for larger pictures, were much loved for their snapshots of popular British bird species.

This book is the fifth Terance James Bond title to be published: all have been partly retrospective in nature and, to some extent, autobiographical or biographical in content. Terry hasn't illustrated anyone else's books, skirting a path followed by many wildlife painters. Unlike Raymond Harris-Ching, he wasn't drawn into the back-breaking effort of providing hundreds of illustrations for a reference work.

In Terry's few published works, he has tended to let the pictures do most of the talking, with this book being unusual thanks to the extended discussion of Terry's early life and of his conservation efforts.

The first book, *Birds: the Paintings of Terance James Bond*, was launched in 1988 by Lutterworth Press of Cambridge. Featuring a striking Peregrine Falcon on the cover, it was subsequently reprinted for the North American market by Athena Press.

In 1992, Dragon's World published *The Terance James Bond Portfolio* in large-format softback. The cover star this time was the humble Wren, while 28 of the artist's favourite species perched on the pages.

Just a year later, the same publisher delivered the weightier *Birds, an Artist's View*, sporting a Kingfisher on the hardback

Song Thrush *(Turdus philomelos)*

UK conservation status: red
Habitat: woodland, scrub, towns
Diet: seeds, invertebrates (especially earthworms), fruit, snails. Ground feeder
Also known as: Mavis or Throstle

This popular member of the Thrush family is an accomplished songster, with each bird having about 100 phrases to repeat. Once a very common sight and sound, numbers are declining rapidly, making it a red list species, with a British population occupying one million territories. The bird is smaller (23cm) and browner than the Mistle Thrush. Song Thrushes are relatively short-lived, typically lasting no more than four years in the wild. Only a fifth of fledglings and fewer than two-thirds of adults survive to breed the following spring. The population decline appears to be the result of a lack of food and the absence of suitable nesting sites, both brought about by intensive farming methods.

Summer is coming, summer is coming
I know it, I know it, I know it
Light again, leaf again, life again, love again,
Yes, my wild little poet
(Alfred, Lord Tennyson: *The Throstle*)

TJB. "This is a very special painting, and for several reasons. In recent years, the Song Thrush has become a less common garden visitor than of old, and always seems to be on the verge of a nervous breakdown. Subservient to most other members of the Thrush family, the Song Thrush has to be extremely canny in order to survive. I have lost count of the number of times I have watched the bird struggle to remove a worm from the lawn, only to be subjected to a mugging by one of the local blackbirds and promptly lose its hard-won meal. Perhaps this is why my wife Jill loves this bird so much. No doubt it was her particular feelings for the Song Thrush that made it her choice when she asked me to paint a picture for a notable birthday. A very special bird for a very special lady!"

Left: Barn Owl plate from Bond's Owls, Danbury Mint

cover and 190 pages rich with pictures and text, a guide to Terry's technique accompanied by many sketches to demonstrate his skill with the pencil.

In 2006, Terry celebrated his 60th birthday in style, with a new book (*A Life in Detail*) and an accompanying exhibition at The Wildlife Art Gallery in Lavenham. The Langford Press volume ran to 180 pages and featured his extremely ambitious painting of ten Puffins on the wrap-around cover.

As mentioned in 'The big day and big decisions', Terry's first one-man exhibition took place in 1971 and has since been followed by a further 21 generally sell-out shows. In 2003 and 2004, he featured in the *Daily Mail*'s 'Not the Turner Prize'

exhibition aimed at more conventional artists swept aside by the move towards 'modern' art. His pictures were selected from an entry of around 10,000 artists to be included in the prestigious show at London's Mall Galleries. On both occasions, Terry's paintings made the top ten.

Several editions of bone china collectables were commissioned and produced by Wedgwood, including the Centenary Celebratory collection for the RSPB. In fact, the cheapest way to 'own a TJB' is via a plate such as the RSPB series or Danbury Mint's 'Bond's Owls' by Wedgwood. Such was the success of these extensive 'limited' editions that there are many examples to be found on the second-hand market at reasonable prices. 🐦

Kingfisher

TJB. "Some paintings have the capacity to evoke certain memories, and this image of a Kingfisher is one such picture. The stones, large and small, were photographed – along with many others – one warm, still evening in North Wales. The location was the out-stream of the huge dam at Nant-y-Moch Reservoir, a wonderful place high in the mountains south of the Snowdon range. As I clambered over and around the rocks of this magical place, the light seemed to get better and better. The result of those few hours of photography has furnished me with many backgrounds for paintings that have been completed during the past ten years – and, hopefully, for several more works in the future."

House Sparrow *(Passer domesticus)*

UK conservation status: red
Habitat: near man
Diet: seeds, also shoots, berries, scraps, some insects;
feeds mostly on the ground
Also known as: Spug

The collective noun for this charming little bird (14cm in length) is 'Host', or 'Tribe', although it is now far harder to justify either, given the dramatic decline in House Sparrow numbers. The trend of housing livestock in inaccessible buildings, plus the mechanisation of grain harvesting and the more effective storage of grain, has reduced the Sparrow's access to food. Nesting sites have also disappeared on farms and in towns, driving down the breeding population from at least 12 million in the 1970s to possibly only a third of that total today. Sadly, Sparrows may be on the conservation red list for some time.

Tell me not of joy; there's none,
Now my little Sparrow's gone
(William Cartwright: *The Dead Sparrow*)

TJB. "'Never take anything for granted'. The old saying has a very pertinent and depressing application regarding the fortunes of this, once one of our most common resident birds. Totally urbanised, the House Sparrow was once regarded as an agricultural pest, a hunting quarry, a delicacy for the table and even as a caged pet. It is quite astounding to think that the British population of the House Sparrow was once estimated at about 25 million. In only 30 years, numbers have crashed and historic colonies of the bird have been reduced by as much as 90 per cent. As discussed earlier, mechanised farming practices and fewer nesting sites have taken their toll, but no one is entirely sure why the downturn has been so severe and so rapid.

"I love these little characters. They are always a joy to paint and, in common with the Robin, can be illustrated within a seemingly endless variety of backgrounds. Familiarity breeds contempt (another well-known adage) but, at close quarters, the cock House Sparrow in full breeding plumage is a handsome bird indeed. Both the paintings on this page reflect the close association with a metropolitan habitat: the clay tiles on the old stables, not far from my studio, are a setting that I have always found fun to paint."

Seeking inspiration

A career devoted to painting native birds, and 'leisure' time dedicated largely to the development and management of the land in Suffolk, has resulted in little time for distractions such as traditional holidays. The Bonds therefore haven't travelled the world in search of exotic species, but have criss-crossed the UK in search of relaxation and inspiration.

Terry doesn't paint on location, like many wildlife artists, but will take home images (either in his head or in his camera) of those special wild places that may eventually form a backdrop for his birds.

His photographic equipment dominates the luggage compartment. Terry has come a long way from the Pentax received from Jill at the time of their wedding in 1970. His latest equipment, which dragged him kicking and screaming into the digital age, helps capture in optimum detail the trees, rocks and water that help put his birds in context.

Few of his often spectacular photographs are actually destined for recreation in acrylic on board. Most are taken just for the sheer pleasure of it, becoming a lasting record of a stunning landscape and providing a different compositional challenge for the artist.

While the trips to the US in the 1980s provided a great opportunity to encounter new species of birds, Terry admits to a sense of mild disappointment that his first sighting of an Osprey should take place in Florida rather than in Scotland. These handsome fish-loving raptors are almost too common a sight in America, while a British sighting still represents a major achievement.

He enjoyed seeing Pelicans and Burrowing Owls while stateside, but got still greater pleasure out of his first Red Kite sighting in North Wales. The tremendous success of the UK Red Kite re-introduction programme means that he can occasionally see them from his back garden. Back in the 1980s, however, it was much more of an occasion.

North Wales has become a happy hunting ground, with several trips bringing the Bonds close to dramatic landscapes, unspoilt woodlands and clear-running rivers. The RSPB reserve at Ynys-hir in the heart of Wales has been a favourite spot, with a good hotel backing conveniently on to its boundary. The dam at Nant-y-Moch reservoir, high in the mountains south of the Snowdon range, has also provided regular inspiration for Terry's paintings.

This part of the country combines Welsh oak woodland with wet grassland and salt marsh. In the spring, the land is carpeted in flowers, with nest boxes playing host to Flycatchers and Redstarts. Summer on the reserve brings wading birds such as Lapwing and Redshank. In the colder winter months, ducks and geese move in.

Cumbria and Scotland rival Wales for the scenery and tranquillity sought by the Bonds when away from the demands of Little Paddock and Terry's studio. Recent years have seen several visits, with the area around Loch Torridon in the Scottish Highlands now a favourite haunt, although Loch Awe in Argyll & Bute was an earlier source of inspiration.

Closer to home, a large number of TJB paintings reflect an enduring love of the Suffolk and North Norfolk coasts, combining wild salt marsh, sandy expanses, working harbours and seaside towns. From Titchwell and Snettisham across to Cley, through the Norfolk Broads to the RSPB's Strumpshaw Fen and down to Minsmere, the region provides many opportunities for the bird enthusiast.

Decaying mooring posts, abandoned crab pots, derelict boats and colourful buoys make tempting subjects to accompany the birds, and Terry's curious obsession with rope has, of course, been discussed earlier!

Every outing is an opportunity for those with a keen eye for the birds. While sitting in a small airport lounge in the French town of Bergerac, having just visited a collector, Terry and Jill remember watching Black Kites hunting along the edges of the runway. Witnessing dozens of these striking birds, Terry admits to feeling like a fraud, as UK-based birdwatchers will probably never catch even a glimpse of a Black Kite.

Traditional rural 'beauty spots' aren't the only, or even necessarily the best, places to see interesting birds or to find inspiration for paintings. Cropping up regularly in TJB pictures

Grey Wagtail
(Motacilla cinerea)

UK conservation status: amber
Habitat: banks of swift streams, lakes
Diet: small invertebrates from ground or fly catching; will hunt in water

The name does this pretty bird a grave disservice, as the slate grey upper parts are accessorised with a distinctive lemon yellow colour under the tail. The tail itself is appreciably longer than that of the Pied and Yellow Wagtails (giving a total length of 18cm), and is therefore prone to more obvious 'wagging'. The birds have expanded gradually into the English lowlands from the northern and western uplands, but they suffer badly in harsh winters. Recent declines have led to the Grey Wagtail's inclusion on the amber list. Data suggest that Britain supports a population of around 38,000 pairs.

TJB. "Running water is a prerequisite for the Grey Wagtail, and very occasionally one of them will visit our ornamental garden pool at home in Suffolk, presumably attracted by the running water that is pumped across the meadow from one of our larger natural ponds. The bird shown in this picture is set in a location not so very far from home. The old ropes were photographed on the River Alde in coastal Suffolk."

are abandoned sea defences, rusting barbed wire, ramshackle gates and collapsing farm buildings.

Terry recalls that his first sighting of a cock Wheatear, looking stunning in full breeding plumage, was at RAF Wattisham just a few miles from his home. On this occasion, the bird was hunting for insects on large areas of concrete serving the airfield. Even now, Terry cannot view a Wheatear without thinking of Mark VI English Electric Lightnings!

It may surprise readers to know that the area around his beloved Suffolk home still represents the greatest source of inspiration for his paintings. Either on his own land, or that of near neighbours, Terry can find consistently the birds and backgrounds that make up his stock in trade. In this book alone, there are numerous local buildings, gates, fences, posts and trees providing ideal perches for many species.

Terry has managed to establish his home and build his career just a few miles from his birthplace. This same small patch of Suffolk has sustained him throughout childhood and adulthood. In return, Terry and Jill have ploughed much of what they have earned back into the land that supports them, closing a perfect circle. 🐦

Spotted Flycatcher
(Muscicapa striata)

UK conservation status: red
Habitat: open woodland, gardens
Diet: mainly flying insects;
hunts from perch

The Spotted Flycatcher is similar in size to the Great Tit (around 14cm long) and bigger than the Pied Flycatcher. It is grey-brown in colour with an off-white breast, streaked with darker grey. This increasingly rare bird likes to perch conspicuously and watch for passing insects, rising up to snaffle them before returning to the perch. Recent dramatic population declines puts the species high on the red list. There are believed to be just 59,000 UK territories.

TJB. "If any bird fits the description LBJ (little brown job), then this summer visitor certainly qualifies. It is a plain dresser and is no great shakes as a singer. However, its ability to catch flying insects on the wing gives it a real 'fast food' diet. During the summer, while these little birds perform aerobatics outside my studio window, one can hear a very definite 'click' as the beak snaps shut on some item of prey. These are not shy characters and are very tolerant of human presence. They will nest against the walls of domestic buildings, behind creepers and ivy, inside hanging baskets and will make good use of suitable nest boxes. Unfortunately, this is another of our delightful regular tourists suffering from an unexplained fall in numbers. We simply do not know why – it certainly cannot be the shortage of flies, spotted or otherwise!"

Lapwing (Vanellus vanellus)

UK conservation status: red
Habitat: pasture, wet
meadow, estuaries
Diet: invertebrates from the
ground; will feed at night under
bright moonlight
Also known as: Peewit, Pewit,
Green Plover, Teuchit,
Hornpie, Flopwing

Thanks go to Chaucer for the rather unfortunate collective, 'a deceit' of Lapwings. He wrote of the *false lapwynge, ful of treacherye,* although it is hard to see how such a delightful bird could have offended him. These 30cm tall birds are now being punished with a worrying 80 per cent decline in numbers since 1960, although large migrant groups can be seen grazing winter fields or flapping lazily over the autumn landscape. This distinctive flight pattern gives the bird its 'proper' name, although Peewit comes close to describing the display call. The UK population is just over 150,000 pairs, putting the species firmly on the conservation red list.

Under the after-sunset sky
Two pewits sport and cry,
more white than is the moon on high
riding the dark surge silently;
more black than earth. Their cry
is the one sound under the sky.
(Edward Thomas: *Two Pewits*)

TJB. "Many of our resident birds have local names that are peculiar to the different regions of this country. I have always known this bird either as the Lapwing, Peewit or Green Plover but, apparently, the bird has as many as 60 colloquial names. Despite the plethora of titles, the Lapwing itself is unfortunately not so plentiful. This is a situation resulting from major changes to agricultural practices and modern farming timetables. Farming in my own area of East Anglia now seems to be centred on the production of cereals, sugar beet and oil seed rape – only one of these crops is now spring-sown. The grazing meadows and damp, unimproved land that was so common 40 years ago is all but a thing of the past. Lapwings require short grass or vegetation in which to nest. The length of the surrounding greenery is critical. If it is too long, the birds are unable to see the approach of any predator. If it is too short, the predators can see them. Cereal crops are suitable if sown in the spring. However, the winter-sown wheat and barley are too established by the time the birds' nesting season arrives. Luckily, we still receive a large number of migrant Lapwings during the winter months, and a visit to locations such as Welney in Cambridgeshire and the RSPB reserves on the Norfolk and Suffolk coasts will reward the birdwatcher with large congregations of Lapwings in company with their close cousin, the Golden Plover."

Part Four

A long and winding road

It was the house of their dreams more than 40 years ago and remains so today. This once modest bungalow in a beautiful part of Suffolk has grown with Terry and Jill Bond, but the plot of land surrounding it has expanded still more rapidly. What in 1977 was an ideal home for two people has since become the perfect sanctuary for dozens of other species.

The road to Little Paddock was, in every sense, long and winding. Not only does the glorified track meander slowly between the Suffolk villages of Boxford and Kersey, but the journey to eventual home ownership in the neighbouring hamlet of Wickerstreet Green was also full of twists and turns.

It wasn't the Bonds' first property but, even before they were married in 1970, it was the one they had set their hearts on. It then took three attempts over two or three years to secure the house – which proved to be just the beginning of an epic real estate adventure spanning three decades.

The importance of the residential garden as a wildlife habitat is now well known, and we are all being encouraged to take nature into account when planning, planting and pruning. In fact, the area covered by our gardens exceeds that of all the British national parks and nature reserves put together. Given that national parks alone account for more than 23,000 square kilometres, we have become important landowners and would-be conservationists.

Terry likes to point out that even the smallest garden can provide close encounters with wildlife on a daily basis. For those not brought up on a farm, the humble back garden is arguably the basis for most people's initial interest in nature.

In the late 1970s, however, precious little thought was given to the use of the garden as a wildlife refuge. Planting to attract insects and birds is a much more recent phenomenon. Most people 30 years ago wanted neat lawns and carefully edged beds, pretty shrubs and bedding plants, a patio for al fresco dining, plus the occasional decorative tree. Perhaps a stone birdbath or a small goldfish pond might have been included as an ornamental, rather than a functional, feature.

Terry and Jill were clearly ahead of the trend with their desire for bird-friendly acreage. They already knew that their land had to serve more than one purpose. Yes, they wanted something pretty to look at, providing a colourful backdrop for the white walls of the bungalow. But they were also aware of the need to attract as many species as possible – and to keep them fed and watered.

For Terry, it was also an attempt to recreate the environment of his youth, when he would roam the farmland at will. He wanted a plot of land, plenty of trees and ideally a pond, to be shared with no one but Jill, their dogs and the wildlife.

Left: aerial view of Little Paddock, showing some of the land acquired since 1977

Little Owl *(Athene noctua)*

UK conservation status: green
Habitat: fields, farmland, towns, open woodland
Diet: mostly earthworms, large invertebrates, small mammals, the occasional small bird; hunts at dawn and dusk
Also known as: Dutch Owl

This small (22cm in height) and appealing owl was introduced to the UK in the 19th century, largely from the Netherlands – although there is evidence that it was once native to Britain. It can be seen in daylight, perching on a branch, telegraph pole or rock, bobbing its head when alarmed. This could be the original 'wise' owl, as its Latin name is from Athene, the Greek goddess of wisdom. Thanks to a taste for earthworms, Little Owls have been known to tumble backwards when fighting to extract their prey from the ground. They nest in disused rabbit holes, as well as in hedgerows, holes in trees and even in haystacks. Low nest sites and their diminutive size leave them vulnerable to attack by domestic cats. The UK population numbers around 8,700 pairs.

TJB. "If a client commissioned a painting of an owl but informed me that they had a limited budget, I would paint one of these! Seriously, if you did have to produce a small painting of an owl, then this would be the one – the Little Owl really is tiny. A mature cock bird is about the same size as a large tin of baked beans and just as volatile! This owl is an introduced species which, over the past 150 years or so, has become integrated into our native avifauna. It is the one member of our resident owl group that can be observed during the day as, unlike most owls, it is not strictly nocturnal."

Ideal home

Living 25 miles apart, courtship between Terry and Jill involved a regular, and increasingly familiar, commute from Ipswich to Assington using the blue Mini Jill had been given by her father. On several such journeys, they passed a bungalow under construction in a meadow on the outskirts of Kersey. Its idyllic location captured their imaginations and they dreamt aloud about one day owning a property 'just like that one'. Jill believes its location was the biggest draw, with the small house nestling gently amid its own plot, surrounded by farmland and just far enough away from the nearest village.

Following their marriage, there had been unsatisfactory skirmishes with the East Anglian property market. The first house in New Buckenham had lasted just 13 months. Their bungalow in Elmsett provided a comfortable home between 1971 and 1977, but Kersey was never far from their thoughts.

Twice they missed out narrowly on securing Little Paddock. Many other couples would have given up, either staying put or looking elsewhere. With their existing home in Elmsett on the market, but not selling, it looked hopeless. Then they received a tip that the Kersey property was again available after a failed sale. Taking a chance, the Bonds made an offer – and immediately found a buyer in Elmsett. In July 1977 they claimed their prize and secured the white bungalow and its three-quarter-of-an-acre plot.

Plans were hatched immediately to transform the small parcel of undeveloped land into an irresistible attraction for local birdlife. Numerous trees and shrubs were planted (rather haphazardly, they now admit), not just to create an attractive garden but also to form a compact conservation area.

Already thinking big, the intrepid pair sought ways to enlarge and improve the plot. One of their neighbours, who fortuitously collected Terry's paintings, owned land that surrounded the garden at Little Paddock. Over time, the Bonds were able to expand the original tract through luck and persistence.

A breakthrough came after a couple of years. Adjacent to the bungalow's original parcel of land was a two-acre, oddly shaped meadow known in Suffolk as a 'dog leg'. This was bought in 1982, at which point the first pond was dug and several hundred native species of tree were planted. With the original garden trees now maturing nicely, the Bonds were well on their way to creating the desired natural habitat for Terry's many feathered friends. 🐦

Left: planting trees at Little Paddock. Below: the Bonds with Twigs and Brambles (sadly now in doggy heaven)

Kingfisher

TJB. "Living near the East Anglian coast, I am blessed with locations that provide endless inspiration for my paintings. On this particular day, Jill and I had decided a trip to Southwold (in Suffolk) was in order. The itinerary included photography, birdwatching, walking and a fish and chip lunch (not necessarily in that order). These old fishing nets and ropes caught my attention, and I spent a happy hour or so photographing the arrangement of colours and textures. As a subject, the Kingfisher was the obvious choice. The colours of the bird and the association of boats and water seemed perfect. Several Kingfishers can be found in this book, but no justification is required as I simply love painting them."

An ill wind

Fate intervened in the shape of the October 1987 'Great Storm', which cut vast swathes through Southern England, damaging or destroying much in its path. The Bonds' more mature trees fell like ninepins, leaving them to face a scene of devastation the following morning. It looked like a major setback, as ten years of blood, sweat and hard cash had been lost in one night.

In this instance, it was an ill wind that blew somebody some good. The damage to the Bonds' plot was overshadowed by the destruction dealt out to an acre of poplar plantation and mere located alongside their 'dog leg' of land. In this instance, the unfortunate owner awoke to the sight of 70 or 80 huge trees scattered across an area of shallow water and wet marsh. Thoroughly depressed by the scale of the necessary clearing-up and replanting, the Bonds' elderly neighbour offered to sell them the land.

In 1988, Terry and Jill set to work restoring the site, de-silting and digging out the mere, importing 2,000 tonnes of topsoil and re-planting trees and shrubs. The storm, which had otherwise caused so much misery, ended up providing a major addition to the would-be wildlife haven.

Five years later, following the death of their much-loved neighbour, the Bonds were offered one of the fields adjacent to the original 'dog leg'. This comprised about five acres and, along one boundary, included a perfect ancient wooded green lane. Now the time had come to move up a gear in terms of the landscaping effort. There was clearly scope for a more serious body of water, some natural woodland and wild flower areas. A small lake was ultimately dug, with a surface area approaching half an acre. Terry was able to apply his engineering skills to an inter-linked water distribution system for irrigation and pond management.

Perhaps in recognition of their efforts, nature lent a helping hand. The pond was complete, but empty. Terry had an exhibition to attend in Lavenham. The heavens opened. Expecting an empty

The scene of devastation after the 1987 'Great Storm'

gallery, the Bonds were greeted with another sell-out. Meanwhile, the torrential rain had completely filled the new pond!

Once water had arrived, there was a clamour of interest from the local wildlife. Terry and Jill remember that, within days of the ponds in the meadows being filled, they were home to water beetles and other aquatic invertebrates. Wood Pigeons and Pheasant arrived to drink, while smaller birds splashed about in the shallows. Within a month, marginal plants were growing.

Securing the additional land had cost the Bonds more than twice the original price of the house and gardens. Adding in the money spent on equipment hire, labour, trees and plants, the overall investment dwarfs that of their initial outlay. However, it has given Terry his trees, his water and far more than the modest one acre he dreamt of. 🐦

Greenfinch *(Carduelis chloris)*

UK conservation status: green
Habitat: woodland, farmland, gardens
Diet: large seeds, cereal grain,
some invertebrates

A popular visitor to the sunflower seed-feeder, the 15cm-high Greenfinch brightens up many gardens now that its natural habitat is under attack. Modern agricultural methods are wiping out the weed seeds that once formed the bird's staple diet, but our generosity is keeping the species alive. There are thought to be around 695,000 territories in the UK. Sociable Greenfinches squabble among themselves and with other garden visitors. They are found in most woodlands and hedges, often close to man.

Amid yon tuft of hazel trees,
that twinkle to the gusty breeze,
behold him perched in ecstasies,
yet seeming still to hover;
There! where the flutter of his wings
upon his back and body flings
shadows and sunny glimmerings,
that cover him all over.
(William Wordsworth: *The Green Linnet*)

TJB. "In complete contrast to the Yellowhammer, this solid-looking member of the finch family has adapted to the rural garden and large city parks as if to the manor born. Literally hundreds of Greenfinches visit my feeding stations during the winter, causing commotion and upset among the titmice. They love peanuts, and the four feeders that are strategically placed around the garden usually require refilling every other day. Greenfinches are typical birds of large overgrown hedgerows, woodland edge and mature gardens. Their diet is based around some of the larger seeds and grain that such habitats provide. Unfortunately, this particular diet renders the birds short of suitable food in the late spring – so keep those feeders going until the end of May if you can."

Flocks of visitors

Created by the Bonds at Little Paddock are a young oak wood, a mixed silver birch and hawthorn plantation, a wildflower meadow complete with the prevalent local species, the original mere plus new, deeper lakes and interlinking channels. There are areas of rough grass and formal lawns. Terry and Jill acquired ancient hedgerows and mature oaks with purchased land, and have fought off many attempts by local farmers to fell trees and rearrange the landscape for easier agricultural access.

The small woodland areas have matured to the extent that many types of birds and insects have taken up residence. The ponds are now home to at least six varieties of dragonfly, plus great crested newts, frog and toad tadpoles, and numerous other invertebrates. The bird count is in excess of 100 species, including occasional VIP visitors such as Red Kite, Little Egret and even a juvenile Osprey that took a fancy to some of Jill's larger goldfish.

Sharing Little Paddock with the Bonds is a representative selection of most of the feathered species found in Eastern England. Tawny Owls and Kestrels nest regularly, while Barn Owls patrol the meadows. More than a decade ago, Terry enlisted the help of friends to erect in the centre of the meadow an old telegraph pole with a nest box attached. A pair of Kestrels promptly took up residence, and they have bred successfully most years since.

While on the subject of birds of prey, Sparrowhawks will often feast on the smaller birds drawn to Little Paddock by the habitat and food sources. More exotic visitors such as Peregrine Falcons, Buzzards and Hobbies can occasionally be spotted overhead.

The many trees play host to all three flavours of British Woodpecker, plus Nuthatch, Tree Creeper, four Titmice

Terry's life-long dream of having somewhere special to work with a view of the land was fulfilled in 1979 when he built his studio

variants and the majority of domestic and some visiting finches. Clouds of Blackbirds scour the lawns in search of worms or fallen fruit, accompanied occasionally by Song and Mistle Thrushes. Winter draws in Fieldfares and Redwings. Yellowhammers and Bramblings compete with House and Tree Sparrows for seed beneath the feeders, joined by the ever-present Robins and Dunnocks.

Game birds pay regular visits, seeking refuge from shotgun pellets or destruction on the roads. Pheasant and Red-Legged Partridge scuttle across the terrace, while clattering through the trees come Wood Pigeon, Collared and Turtle Doves.

Family *Corvidae* is well represented by opportunistic Magpie and Jackdaw raids, particularly when eggs or chicks are in abundance. While hardly living in an ocean-front property, the Bonds have also had their own rather unwelcome Cormorant!

Little Paddock is no longer the most appropriate name for a bungalow nestling among ten acres of woodland, water,

Great Spotted Woodpecker

(Dendrocopos major)

**UK conservation status: green
Habitat: forest,
woodland, gardens
Diet: mostly insects under bark**

Britain's most familiar Woodpecker, the Great Spotted, is Blackbird-sized (22cm high) and very striking in appearance, with its black-and-white coat and red cap. The bird has an undulating flight and spends most of its time clinging to tree trunks and branches. Peanut feeders have become increasingly popular, bringing these delightful birds to gardens throughout the UK. The population is put at around 41,000 pairs. The drumming sound made by the bird is caused by 10 to 40 strikes of the beak per second against timber. No wonder they need shock-absorbent tissue at the base of the skull.

TJB. "Ask me to paint a Woodpecker and I will immediately begin to fantasise about the quantity of tree trunk that I can include in the composition. Very often, I will use the subject of a painting purely as an excuse to illustrate the rest of the picture. However, in this instance, the client made it clear that I was to paint within a certain budget and that the bird was to be the main focus of the picture – hence this compact study of a Great Spotted Woodpecker. Perhaps next time I will be able to indulge my passion and include a few feet of decrepit tree trunk with all its associated worm holes and the like. The most important thing, of course, is to satisfy the client's request, and I am happy to say that the recipient of this particular work was delighted."

grass and shrubs. In the long, dry summer of 2009, it was re-christened temporarily 'Little Desert' as plant life withered and died, ponds evaporated and leaves tumbled months ahead of schedule.

The previous year, badgers tore up the lawns, showing a complete lack of appreciation for the efforts made to preserve their natural habitat. Laying new turf simply provided a fresh challenge for worm-hungry *Meles meles*. Another

ungrateful member of the *Mustelidae* family, the otter, harvests the goldfish and Koi in Jill's pool, enjoying the handy sushi establishment on its doorstep.

Serious fish-keeping may now have been abandoned, after the depravations of the otters and visiting Cormorant, but Kingfishers will still fly in for the goldfish fry. While the owners of Little Paddock love to feed the birds, it can sometimes get out of hand!

Pied Wagtail *(Motacilla alba)*

UK conservation status: green
Habitat: open country, often near water
Diet: small invertebrates from ground or fly catching
Also known as: Willy Wagtail

For many people, this is the most familiar Wagtail, rushing around supermarket car parks or garden lawns in pursuit of insects. It is a charming black and white bird, always in formal dress that seems to accentuate the extreme 'wagging' of the tail. It calls frequently during its undulating flight, and Pied Wagtails (which are around 18cm in length) will often gather at dusk to form large roosts in city centres. There are thought to be just over 290,000 British territories.

TJB. "Black and white birds are good news for the bird artist, as the monochromatic plumage of species such as the Pied Wagtail and Pied Flycatcher will integrate well with practically any other colour. Painting ropes is a challenge that I find hard to resist. The texture, shape and contortions of a length of discarded rope, with its associated shadows, are a tricky but a very satisfying thing to tackle. Ropes appear frequently in my paintings and I recall, as a very young boy at primary school, that my nickname was 'Bondage' (don't ask!). The ropes in this painting were photographed at the old harbour of Southwold in Suffolk. Using the convenient privilege of artistic licence, I decided to alter the colour of a section of the rope in order to introduce another key pigment into the composition. Elsewhere in this book is another painting of a Pied Wagtail also incorporating a great slab of red and, now I come to think about it, the composition also includes another piece of rope!"

Bullfinch (Pyrrhula pyrrhula)

UK conservation status: amber
Habitat: orchards, forest,
woodland, farmland
Diet: seeds of fleshy fruits,
buds, shoots

Still not popular with orchard owners, thanks to their habit of eating the buds of fruit trees, Bullfinches are highly attractive birds most often spotted at woodland edges and given away by a mournful call. The male bird (16cm high) sports a flamboyant bright pinkish-red waistcoat, wears a grey coat and black cap, and boasts a white rump. A fleeting glimpse of that splash of white, plus the sad call, may be the closest most people get to the most striking of British finches. In the summer, Bullfinches in Britain occupy almost 160,000 territories.

The honours of his ebon poll
Were brighter than the sleekest mole;
His bosom of the hue
With which Aurora decks the skies,
When piping winds shall soon arise
To sweep up all the dew.
(William Cowper: *On the Death of Mrs Throckmorton's Bullfinch*)

TJB. "For a few months after leaving school, while waiting to start at engineering college, I worked on a local fruit farm. This was during the early 1960s and, in those less than enlightened times, attitudes towards certain species of wildlife were less tolerant than today. In those days, if you ran a commercial orchard, the Bullfinch was viewed as the enemy. Indeed, the damage that these beautiful finches could inflict on certain types of fruit trees during the spring had to be seen to be believed. Pear trees seem to be the favourite target and, as a result, thousands of the birds were trapped or shot as a matter of course. Circumstances have now changed. Apart from the scarcity of large fruit farms in the UK, the birds themselves are also much less widespread. Thankfully, in common with all other small birds, they are now protected by law. That shocking pink plumage flaunted by the cock bird is a pigment that I cannot recall having to use on any other subject. Despite that loud colour, Bullfinches are quiet and rather discreet little birds with no real song to speak of. They maintain a low profile and, considering their persecution in the past, you cannot really blame them."

Part Five

A constant challenge

A born countryman, Terry can now patrol his territory and the neighbouring farmland, keeping a watchful eye on the species that provide his income – as well as bringing to book anyone caught abusing the environment. Farmers seeking consolation over inconsiderate nest sites or poorly positioned trees can expect little sympathy!

At least once a day (and more often twice), Terry walks three-and-a-half miles over his land and around the adjoining farm. Every day throws up something new or interesting. If TJB gets his timing right, he can walk through his own dog leg of land, with its self-sown oaks, and spot the resident Tawny Owls sitting in the young trees prior to their nightly hunt.

For the Bonds, there are no swimming pools and tennis courts, in spite of open spaces that put wealthier neighbours to shame. You could risk a dip in the mere or the ponds, but you would be sharing the murky water with forms of life that don't wear Speedos.

One thing Terry and Jill learnt early on is that a wilderness needs plenty of managing. Left to its own devices, the land would suffer. Plenty of species would prosper, but many more would be suffocated. Fallen trees cannot always be left to rot – and some have no respect for power lines.

Ponds cannot be left indefinitely without dredging, replanting or refilling. Streams can get blocked and overflow, while wildlife can occasionally be destructive (like the badgers). Meadows need cutting regularly so that wild flowers can flourish and fend off the grasses. It is a continuous process of land management that calls for devotion, time, money and heavy machinery.

Both human occupants of Little Paddock have had to learn several new skills in order to deal with the challenges of habitat management. Ironically for Terry, having earlier turned his back on earth-moving plant as a career (see 'First sale to first show', page 16), he now admits to an enthusiasm for either using the machines or watching the professionals at work.

Over the years, he has hired small diggers, dumpers, excavators and various other 'toys' in order to landscape and improve the plot. When it came to digging the larger ponds and sorting out the storm damage, he brought out the big guns, with 'man-size' machinery drafted in. "There is something fascinating about an experienced operator using a 25-tonne excavator and accompanying vehicles to create ponds, lift fallen trees or remove debris," says Terry.

The wild flower areas and walkways also have to be maintained, as do the hedges and trees. The year during which Terry and Jill planted their woodland was one of the driest on record. It was followed by two more 'dusters', and the Bonds resorted

Left: digging out the mere; Right: ponds can be very demanding...

to pumping water out of one of the ponds by the bungalow, filling 60 five-gallon buckets and, with tractor and trailer, transporting the contents to the meadow to water 350 new trees. This was repeated every ten days for three summers, and they lost just one tree...

If Terry is chained to his easel, conjuring up visions of birds at rest and play, Jill will be fighting through the undergrowth, trying to tame the landscape. The formal gardens around the house arguably provide light relief compared with the constant demands of the woodland, meadows and lakes, but coping with both the cultivated and the wild at Little Paddock is easily a full-time job. However, Jill also has to keep the house in good order, feed and water the artist, manage his business affairs and – perhaps most importantly – keep his bow ties spotless! ✎

Wren *(Troglodytes troglodytes)*

UK conservation status: green
Habitat: forest, woodland, undergrowth
Diet: insects, especially beetles, spiders;
usually feeds close to ground

Britain's most common breeding species, the Wren is so secretive that many never even catch a glimpse of this tiny (10cm) brown bird with the loud voice and scolding call. Other features are a narrow pointed beak and stubby tail that often points skywards. The birds occupy more than eight million territories - although harsh winters can reduce dramatically the number of birds.

Among the dwellings framed by birds
In field or forest with nice care,
Is none that with the little Wren's
In snugness may compare.
(William Wordsworth, *The Wren's Nest*)

TJB. "In spite of rumours to the contrary, the Wren is not our smallest resident bird species. That accolade must go to the still-smaller Goldcrest, weighing in at about 6 grams, or half that of the Wren. Another misconception is that the Wren is somehow related to the titmouse family, no doubt as a result of our Victorian predecessors referring to the bird as a 'tit wren'. Actually, the Wren is in a genus all of its own and possesses one of the largest scientific names on the list, *Troglodytidae troglodytidae*. At the time of writing, we are just coming out of a second consecutive 'proper' winter, as some locals in the village remind me. Weather such as this is bad news for small birds, but hopefully Wren numbers will recover as they are capable of two broods per season – each containing up to eight eggs. During severe winters, nest boxes are literally a lifesaver for these little birds. As many as 40 have been recorded huddled together to conserve warmth and to secure a degree of safety from predators."

Room with a view

In their first two (temporary) homes at New Buckenham and Elmsett, Terry was forced to use a spare bedroom as his makeshift studio. Even at Little Paddock for the first two years, the dining room was pressed into service as the artist's workspace. In 1979, having drawn up the plans and had permission granted, the Bonds began the creation of Terry's studio, thus completing a life-long dream of having somewhere special to work with a view of the land. Terry carried out the work himself, as he did with subsequent additions to the property, customising the original bungalow to suit his and Jill's particular requirements.

Terry's new studio at Little Paddock under construction in 1979

Most newly married couples buy a home, only to move onward and upwards as circumstances change. More money, more family members or simply a desire for change drive most people up the property ladder. As Terry's painting career took off, he and Jill could have traded up for something bigger.

Instead, the practical side of TJB expressed itself through ambitious home improvement efforts that yielded more space and added 'mod cons'. Natural caution regarding debt, coupled with the uncertainty of painting-sourced cashflow, meant that Terry and Jill stayed loyal to their dream home.

An early decision not to raise a family no doubt made it easier to ignore the temptations of a bigger house. Given Terry's commitment to a potentially precarious existence and

Jill's desire to provide the necessary support, the addition of children could have spoiled the dream. However, a succession of five Labradors were for many years much loved members of the household.

To understand fully the reluctance to move, it is necessary to experience the pleasure of a truly great location. Surrounded by productive farmland, quiet country roads and within reach of charming towns and villages, Little Paddock has everything but nouveau riche 'bling'. There is certainly plenty of that in the neighbourhood, as expensive second homes proliferate. In spite of profits to be made, the Bonds are staying put until the land management becomes too big a burden. 🐦

Nuthatch

TJB. "This little bird turns up several times in this book; I doubt I will ever tire of painting this stunning woodland resident. This particular painting is quite special. We planted the two silver birches illustrated here some 16 years ago in our meadow (along with several hundred others) and they have now acquired a degree of maturity that makes them attractive to many species of small birds. A quick glance through this book will show that I love trees. There you have it – I'm a self-confessed tree hugger! This is an elaborate composition, and one of my all-time favourite images. Fortunately, it now hangs in a client's house not too many miles from my studio. This gives me the chance to renew my acquaintance with the painting on a regular basis. All too often, when my birds have flown, I never see them again."

House Sparrow

TJB. "From an artist's point of view, the House Sparrow opens up endless opportunities regarding composition. Bound inextricably with the activities of urban man, the bird can be found worldwide, taking advantage of human habitation. Having said that, this is the one sparrow painting that has departed from my usual order. For a start, I have painted the female (not my usual practice) and have deliberately kept the painting uncomplicated. The setting could be anywhere except that, of course, the ear of wheat hints at an agricultural location. This work has been executed within a very limited range of pigments typical of my favourite colours."

Swallow *(Hirundo rustica)*

UK conservation status: amber
Habitat: open country, commonly
near water, farmland
Diet: flying insects

Before the wonders of bird migration were appreciated fully, it was thought that Swallows hibernated in winter. We now know that these delicate high-fliers commute to and from southern Africa. Numbers have been falling due to loss of habitat both in Africa and in the UK, hence the inclusion on the amber list. Recent data suggest that around 680,000 British territories are occupied each summer by Swallows. Natural predators are few and far between, thanks to the agility and speed of this 18cm-long bird, although Hobbies and Sparrowhawks can take them on the wing.

The swallow of summer, she toils all the summer
A blue-dark knot of glittering voltage,
A whiplash swimmer, a fish of the air.
(Ted Hughes: *Work and Play*)

TJB. "One Swallow does not a summer make! When I began work on these notes, this certainly seemed to be the case. My local Swallows arrived in early April 2010, and by the end of the week we were experiencing heavy snow accompanied by bitter, easterly winds. As is often the case, spring seemed to arrive late in East Anglia, with blackthorn blossom just coming to an end as the hawthorn was in full bloom – something I hadn't seen in many years. However, summer arrived eventually and provided the inspiration for this painting. Late one June evening, walking the edge of water meadows on the North Norfolk coast, I observed the Swallows resting on fence wires surrounding a meadow. From this vantage point, the birds were hawking out low over the grass hunting for insects disturbed by the livestock."

Three score and five

Terance James Bond

Planning for this volume began more than a year before publication. A significant milestone was looming, namely my 65th birthday. As well as cake, I fancied a show. If there was to be an exhibition, why not another book? It all sounded so simple 12 months ahead of the event. After all, the gallery only needed 30-40 new paintings. At an average of three a month, I had plenty of time, didn't I?

Of course, I would need to fit in some previously agreed commissions, produce paintings needed for the annual calendar, write up a couple of hundred words per image for the book, sort through and make selections from five years of 'older' pictures, get everything photographed, celebrate Christmas, help Jill keep on top of Little Paddock duties...

There is no particular theme for the exhibition. I don't do themes. Instead, I try and paint the best pictures I can of popular species so that as many people as possible will see something they like. In addition, there are a few self-indulgences, such as the very large works featuring a Tawny Owl, Goshawk and Little Owl. I hope that these provide the 'wow' factor, as they are among the most demanding pictures I have ever created.

Each of my paintings takes a surprising amount of time to complete, with the gestation period matching the size of the work and the degree of complexity. It doesn't take a mathemetical genius to work out that I must produce some smaller, simpler pieces in order to fill the gallery's walls in time. Fortunately, such pictures tend to be popular with collectors and first-time buyers alike.

Simple doesn't have to mean small. I have chosen to turn back the clock and produce some bird studies, which are a throwback to earlier years in my career when I focused much more on the bird than on its environment. Given the vast amount of detail included in the larger works, it was a pleasant change to devote such a large proportion of my time exclusively to the birds.

The Peregrine Falcon (page 77) is a good example of how a 'stripped down' picture can still make a big statement. At the other end of the study spectrum, however, come my so-called 'tinies'. In recent exhibitions, I have tended to include several smaller pictures for those without the wall space or wallet space for my more generously proportioned works. While generally around 12 inches by 8 inches (in old money), they tended to feature plenty of background as well as the bird.

This time around, I have decided to ring the changes with a series of small bird studies, containing popular species in all their glory, but set against a neutral background. The finished painting doesn't therefore need to be much bigger than the bird itself, with the result that these are the tiniest originals I have produced in decades.

There are three main groups making up my mini-portfolio of tinies, namely the much-maligned Warblers (often misrepresented merely as small brown jobs), the rather more familiar Titmice (including Scotland's own favourite, the Crested Tit) and my so-called 'Wheat' collection featuring two flavours of Sparrow (I cannot resist them), the ever-popular Chaffinch and the winter-visiting Brambling.

Every bit as much love and care goes into each 'tiny' as into the grander paintings. My fondness for the most humble of garden birds is well known, and it is absolutely no hardship to produce another Tree Sparrow.

So, there you have it – an exhibition designed to please bird-lovers, TJB collectors and, hopefully, innocent passers-by alike. The production of my babies took the usual nine months, but at least I was spared the morning sickness...

This publication could so easily have been simply a show catalogue. Just think of how much time, effort and money that would have saved! However, there were some cracking pictures painted and sold since the last exhibition. How unfair that none would get the chance to grace the pages of a book.

The biography wasn't my idea but, once suggested by author Alan and his wife Marion, who was I to argue? With luck, you will have found it interesting. However, if your own life has been more exciting, you can just enjoy the pictures. Where the 65 years have gone is a mystery, and I have demanded a recount. After all, squeezing in a few more years could have meant a bigger book. Oh well, time to think about the next picture. In the meantime, where is that cake? 🖋

The 65th birthday exhibition

Redstart

(Phoenicurus phoenicurus)

UK conservation status: amber
Habitat: woodland
**Diet: largely insects, butterfly/
beetle larvae, spiders**
Also known as: Firetail

Like a titivated Robin, this 14cm-high summer tourist has a red breast but sports a smart slate-grey coat, black face and wings, and an orange rump. The female and young birds look dull in comparison. There is much 'bobbing' and quivering of the tail, but they are still a rare sight for most people – although they once nested in towns. Unlike Robins, they are not regular garden visitors, keeping off the ground and skulking in oak woodlands and hedgerows. Sadly, they are included on the amber list, as numbers have been falling – particularly on the Continent. The UK nesting population appears to be shrinking, although some believe that their breeding grounds are simply becoming more scattered. Recent data suggest that the UK population is now around 100,000 pairs.

TJB. "This is another of our summer visitors that I always associate with photographic and birdwatching trips to Wales and Cumbria, as the deciduous woodland of these uplands and valleys are a regular haunt of the Redstart. In case you are confused as to why a bird with a red tail isn't called a 'red finish', the name derives apparently from the old English word 'Steort' for tail. It is that fantastic red tail that first catches the eye as the bird flies away. If afforded the opportunity to observe the bird stationary and up close, the true beauty is revealed. The Redstart is another of our woodland migrants that is rather selective in its choice of habitat; the sessile oak woods of the west are preferred to the more pedunculate-biased oak woods of the east. The Pied Flycatcher is of a similar persuasion."

Yellowhammer
(Emberiza citrinella)

UK conservation status: red
Habitat: grassland, farmland
Diet: grass seeds, cereal grain,
some invertebrates
Also known as: Yellow Bunting

Children's author Enid Blyton made famous the description of the Yellowhammer's song, 'little bit of bread and no cheese'. The song may be distinctive, but the bird itself is more so. Males are unmistakeable, with a bright yellow head and underparts, a brown back streaked with black, and a chestnut rump. While the 16cm-high bird can be found across Britain, it is far less common in the north and west. Becoming a more familiar sight in country gardens when food is scarce, the Yellowhammer is another bird species in decline, requiring its inclusion on the red list. In the UK, Yellowhammers are thought to occupy around 790,000 territories.

In early spring, when winds blow chilly cold,
The Yellowhammer, trailing grass, will come
To fix a place and choose an early home,
with yellow breast and head of solid gold.
(John Clare: *The Yellowhammer*)

TJB. "This is a bird that for me will always have strong associations with the countryside, and with farmland in particular. I have lasting teenage memories of this striking bird on my parents' farm and, while heathland and the gorse-covered coastal regions are also popular habitats, I will always think of the farm as the Yellowhammer's true home. This is another of our resident rural species that is in trouble. Winter stubbles that used to provide the birds with foraging during hard times are now a thing of the past in the east of England. Grain is harvested in bulk and stored in vermin-proof silos, or transported away from the farm at harvest-time. This 'high-tech' and efficient modern farming practice does this lovely bird no favours. During really cold weather, especially when there are several weeks of snow cover, groups of Yellowhammers venture into the garden under our feeders to join the ranks of Chaffinches, but this is not a regular occurrence for this truly rural small bird."

Tawny Owl

TJB. "Earlier in this book (see page 37), I have made it plain as to how much affection I have for this particular owl, so I will resist the temptation to wax lyrical again. However, I would like to offer a short discourse on why I painted this picture and why, at the time of writing, it remains my all-time favourite work. The fact that it combines Tawny Owls and trees provides a strong hint. This mature oak is situated on a boundary hedge adjacent to the farm walk that I take every day. On this particular frosty January afternoon, the tree looked wonderful with the late winter sun bringing out every shape and texture of the bark. On this occasion, there was no wind, nothing moved, creating the sort of beautiful winter's day that demands a long walk. I knew, when eventually I got around to painting the tree, that the Tawny Owl would be the subject. I would like to think that this lovely lady is about to start her evening's hunting, but has been distracted momentarily by the viewer of the painting. This is a large work and, as with all my subjects, the owl is painted life-size. If I remember correctly, the piece took more than three months to complete and now hangs in a prime position on one of our dining-room walls, with the perhaps hungry bird surveying our meal-time guests. Each time I look at the painting I am reminded of that cold, still day in January. Sometimes, for me, everything in a painting just works."

Pied Wagtail

TJB. "Red is one of those colours that is referred to in artistic parlance as 'hot'. The artist or photographer has therefore to exercise a degree of restraint when including this most vibrant of pigments in any composition. Technically speaking, it requires only a small area of bright red to lift an image; just a subtle hint to bring a part of the painting alive. I am not quite sure what happened, but I seem to have thrown caution to the wind in this picture. The old boat was hauled up on the foreshore at Southwold harbour and, despite it appearing to be a total wreck, some enterprising owner had given it a coat of paint and was offering it for sale. I was nearly tempted, but satisfied myself with a few photographs instead. Have I overdone the red? I think not, as I am happy with the result. Just to be on the safe side, perhaps I will include a pair of sunglasses in the selling price..."

Kingfisher

TJB. "School holidays, at least summer holidays, coincided with the onset of harvest activities on our family farm. The harvest was a much longer and more prolonged event in the 1950s and '60s than the highly mechanised affair it is today. As a result, spare time was at a premium, with visits to the coast a rare treat. Nowadays, I am drawn to the Suffolk and Norfolk coastal regions with much greater frequency. Photography is the main explanation for this attraction. Old fishing boats, decrepit gangways and decaying mooring posts hold an endless fascination. Most of the main bird reserves in East Anglia are situated either on, or adjacent to, the coast. Therefore, a lot of my bird watching close to home takes place 'on the edge', so to speak. This mooring post, with its amazing collection of ropes, old and new, was photographed on a fresh-water creek in South Norfolk. The tangle and haphazard arrangement of redundant and fresh ropes again proved irresistible. A seemingly odd connection occurs to me here. While walking and photographing in North Wales, I became equally fascinated by the remains of old and rusty wire incorporated with newer sections on many of the old posts around the sheep enclosures. It seems that once a section of wire or rope has come to the end of its useful life, it is replaced with a newer piece and the old bits are just left where they are. Over several years, the whole thing builds up to a mass of interesting and complex patterns that are great fun to paint but which, at the same time, add a degree of timelessness to the post. The subject of this painting, the Kingfisher, is probably only a couple of years old. No doubt some of the ropes on this post have lasted many Kingfisher lifetimes."

Peregrine Falcon *(Falco peregrinus)*

UK conservation status: green
Habitat: moorland, heathland, coastal cliffs and cities
Diet: birds, taken in the air, often after a spectacular stoop

The literal name of this spectacular raptor is 'Pilgrim Falcon', with the Latin title coming from the first-century philosopher, outcast and wanderer Peregrinus Proteus. In the Middle Ages, when falconry was at its zenith, the birds weren't taken from their nests when young and flightless, but were caught on their passage from their breeding-place – hence the term 'pilgrim'. The 42cm-high Peregrine Falcon was among the first bird of prey introduced into British falconry in around the 6th century. The rocky cliffs and uplands of Britain are good places to spot the birds in the breeding season, although city-centre buildings are becoming increasingly popular nesting sites. Almost a fifth of Europe's Peregrines are found in the UK (around 1,400 pairs), giving us a special responsibility to protect this wonderful bird. They are still threatened by illegal persecution, particularly on grouse moors. Scotland isn't therefore the best place to find living birds.

TJB. "One of nature's most efficient killing machines, operating at up to 15,000 feet and armed with weapons capable of bringing down a variety of targets. Known for a diving speed of up to 175mph, it can provide 15 years of active service.' A description of a military aircraft, perhaps? You might be forgiven for thinking so but, in fact, it sums up the Peregrine Falcon beautifully. It is not the biggest of the falcon group, but it is one very impressive flying machine – with all the attributes that make up a perfect predator. It played a pivotal role in the worldwide ban on certain agricultural pesticides and chemicals, something that has assisted its recovery, with numbers now approaching a level not seen in Britain for 70 years. The bird has the potential to be highly successful, as all it requires is a supply of avian food and somewhere to raise a brood. Nesting locations can vary from the precipitous cliffs of north-west Scotland to high-rise office blocks in central London. The Peregrine is a wonderful bird to paint, to observe and simply to be in close proximity to. Seeing one of these beautiful falcons is an experience not to be forgotten. The bird shown here is a mature male, referred to in falconry terms as a 'tiercel', derived from the Latin *tertius*, or a third, roughly the proportion by which the male Peregrine is smaller than the female."

Small study images

TJB. "My paintings are undertaken for various reasons. For example, a client will commission a certain species in a particular setting and probably in a certain price range. On the other hand, I will often paint something prompted by an over-riding desire to illustrate a particular subject and, inevitably, this is how one of my large and complicated set-pieces evolves. The idea of spending weeks or months on a large painting has always appealed, and the challenge of illustrating life size a complex section of tree trunk or a water and stone combination is very exciting. Somehow the detailing of a large area of a painting's background brings about a feeling of 'completeness' in a work. However, at the other end of the scale, I will produce small images that are basically a study of the bird with just a hint of the background or environment that would be appropriate to the species. To use a culinary metaphor, these are my 'palate cleansers'. The thought that I can sit down in the studio at the beginning of the week and complete one of these 'tiddlers' in a few days is very satisfying, and one or two paintings of this type are usually undertaken following weeks on a much larger and more complex work. There are also financial and practical considerations, of course – little paintings represent a smaller investment for the client and are easily accommodated in areas where it would be impossible to hang a large picture. Over the next few pages I have included several representations of what I have always described as my 'tinies'.

Chaffinch *(Fringilla coelebs)*
UK conservation status: green (5.6m territories)
Habitat: forest, woodland, farmland, gardens
Diet: invertebrates in summer, otherwise mostly seeds

Brambling *(Fringilla montifringilla)*
UK conservation status: green (920,000 birds)
Habitat: open birch/conifer woodland
Diet: seeds, berries; in summer invertebrates

The 'Wheat' collection:
Chaffinch, Brambling, Tree Sparrow, House Sparrow

"Modern farming is now a highly efficient and technology-led industry. In my youth, things were a little more 'agricultural'. There was always less tidying up, and most operations on the land and around the buildings always left evidence of recent activity, usually in the form of discarded grain and heaps of chaff-infused straw left over from threshing. The four species illustrated here were some of the most common of the small seed-eating species that, as a young birdwatcher, I would have been familiar with – although, to be completely honest, the Brambling was always an exciting and less common winter visitor (our local farm workers referred to it as the 'Swedish Chaffinch'). If you had suggested to any keen ornithologist in the 1950s that the Tree Sparrow, for instance, would be virtually absent from farmland in 30 years, they would have found it inconceivable. Unfortunately, just such a situation exists today. House Sparrows in those days were so plentiful as to be classed as vermin by farmers and gardeners and, as a result, suffered from relentless persecution. How things have changed..."

Tree Sparrow *(Passer montanus)*
UK conservation status: red (68,000 territories)
Habitat: open woodland, farmland, towns, near man
Diet: mostly seeds (from plants and ground)

House Sparrow *(Passer domesticus)*
UK conservation status: red (4m pairs)
Habitat: near man
Diet: seeds, also shoots, berries, scraps, some insects

Sedge Warbler
(Acrocephalus schoenobaenus)
UK conservation status: green (320,000 territories)
Habitat: reedbed, marshes
Diet: insects; berries in autumn

Reed Warbler
(Acrocephalus scirpaceus)
UK conservation status: green (91,000 pairs)
Habitat: reedbed, scrub
Diet: insects and spiders, also small snails

Warblers

TJB. "Almost without exception, the many warblers on the British List have one thing in common – they are all migrant species as far as the UK is concerned, and they are associated with the warmer days of spring and summer. The four individuals illustrated here are all related and dovetail very neatly into their respective niche habitats. The Sedge and Reed Warblers' appellations indicate fairly accurately the habitat they frequent although, strictly speaking, the latter isn't exclusive to sedge beds – overgrown, damp ditches and field margins suit the species just as well. On first hearing the song of these two warblers, you could be forgiven for thinking they were singing the same tune. However, there are subtle differences in the repertoire once the listener becomes familiar with the dual repetitive song. One thing that helps distinguish the two is the very useful habit adopted by the 'Sedgie' of singing from an exposed perch; the Reed Warbler, on the other hand, chatters away from deep in the reed bed and is usually hard to spot.

Wood Warbler
(Phylloscopus sibilatrix)
UK conservation status: red (17,000 males)
Habitat: forest
Diet: insects and other invertebrates, some fruit

Blackcap
(Sylvia atricapilla)
UK conservation status: green (910,000 territories)
Habitat: forest, open woodland, towns
Diet: in summer, insects, otherwise fruit

"If you think the songs of the Sedge and Reed Warblers are similar, then try to differentiate between those of the Garden Warbler and Blackcap! After years of 'bird listening', these summer visitors can still catch me out. The Blackcap is one of our first real songsters to arrive in the spring, although it has become evident that reasonable numbers of Blackcaps now over-winter in the UK, possibly birds from the northern regions of the species' distribution. It is a very confiding bird, choosing to serenade from low vegetation and hedgerow shrubs – and often allowing close encounters of the birdwatching kind! Its companion on this page, the Wood Warbler, always sings from the leaf canopy in a very specialised arboreal habitat, namely the sessile oak woodlands of Wales and the western wooded valleys of the UK. The bird is a little cracker, sporting a beautiful lime green and yellow outfit and with a very distinctive song, delivered as a falling crescendo from somewhere about 60 feet above your head."

Great Tit
(Parus major)
UK conservation status: green (2m territories)
Habitat: forest, woodland, towns, gardens
Diet: invertebrates & spiders; seeds & fruit in winter

Blue Tit
(Cyanistes caeruleus)
UK conservation status: green (3.3m territories)
Habitat: woodland, scrub, gardens
Diet: insects & spiders; seeds & fruit in winter

Titmice

TJB. "Sitting in my studio writing these notes, I can see three of the titmice illustrated here busy on the seed and nut feeders in the garden. Familiarity breeds contempt, so they say, but I have yet to meet anybody who does not exhibit a real degree of affection for the most common members of the 'parus' family. Blue and Great Tits will feed on peanuts and the fat balls that we provide as if the food was the most natural thing available. They are omnivorous in their feeding habits, so insects, fruit and berries will form a major part of their diet. The Coal Tit is more specialised and will seek out over-wintering insects and their eggs, but also finds it hard to resist the occasional peanut. Coal Tits do, in fact, prefer a coniferous habitat and are generally private diners, removing an item of food from the feeder and retiring to a secluded part of the garden to finish the meal. The introduction and planting of ornamental conifers, large and small, benefited this lovely bird enormously.

Crested Tit
(Lophophanes cristatus)
UK conservation status: amber (2,400 pairs)
Habitat: coniferous or mixed woodland
Diet: mostly insects and spiders

Coal Tit
(Periparus ater)
UK conservation status: green (600,000 territories)
Habitat: woodland, gardens
Diet: insects & spiders; seeds in winter

"Unless you happen to live in a particular part of the Scottish Highlands, it is unlikely that the Crested Tit will turn up on your local bird table – these handsome little birds are restricted to their natural habitat of the ancient pine woodlands of Scotland. Their diet is practically the same as that of other Titmice family members, and there is no doubt that they will visit feeding stations in their locale if provided. In recent history, the suffix 'titmouse' has been applied to several small birds that are not actually true titmice; our Victorian forefathers tended to refer to any small bird as a titmouse. In fact, to qualify for true membership of the 'Titmice Club', you have to be a 'hole nester' – suitable openings in trees, old woodpecker holes and the like are the natural nesting sites for the six members of our resident titmice species. However, as we all know, the birds will take readily to purpose-built nest boxes as long as they are located in suitable places."

Kingfisher

TJB. "Around 18 years ago, we decided to excavate a large pond in our newly acquired meadow. At the time, we considered seriously asking the machinery operator to build a vertical section of bank on one side in the hope that we might encourage a Kingfisher to take up residence. Unfortunately, as the soil was predominantly heavy clay-based loam, we felt that the construction of a four feet-high bank would not be very stable and that the material wouldn't be easy for the birds to burrow into. Nevertheless, not to be deterred, a compromise was adopted. Several posts were sunk into the pond in strategic areas of the water to see if the birds would visit and use these prominent perches from which to fish. Unbelievably, our first Kingfisher arrived within a few weeks! In order to increase the chances of success, the pond was stocked with common rudd and roach fry, both species that breed prolifically and would not cause a great problem to the rest of the invertebrates in the pond. As well as encouraging the Kingfisher, the occasional Grey Heron and Cormorant also drop in for a light snack."

Nuthatch

TJB. "All the ornithological books I have read relating to the Nuthatch emphasise the amazing acrobatics of this wonderful bird during its search for insects and grubs. It has an ability to negotiate tree trunks and branches with a gravity-defying ease. It seems that only British birds adopt the familiar head-down attitude, with most Nuthatches equally happy travelling up branches. I have to admit that this unique posture is one that I choose for the majority of my Nuthatch paintings. However, while penning these notes, I decided to illustrate a bird going in the opposite direction for a change. It turned out well, and appears on page 92 of this book. The painting here shows the bird heading south on an old willow trunk. My inclination to include plenty of tree in my paintings is well known. This specimen is located in a damp corner of my meadow, and parts of it have figured in previous works. Unfortunately, willows mature very quickly. This adds to their interest as a subject, but who knows how much longer this old friend will remain upright? During 33 years at Little Paddock, Jill and I have recorded 115 bird species on our land, but only twice have I seen a Nuthatch – perhaps due to a lack of really ancient hole-ridden trees required for nesting. Hopefully, one or two of the redundant Woodpecker holes in some of our larger trees may appeal eventually to this arboreal specialist."

Barn Owl *(Tyto alba)*

UK conservation status: amber
Habitat: open country, farmland, water meadows
Diet: small mammals (mice, bank voles, shrews), some small birds
Also known as: Screech Owl, Billy Wix, Ginny Ollit

Amber list status may not be enough for this wonderful but endangered bird, with habitat loss and lack of prey leading to an alarming decline. The most recent estimates suggest a UK population of just 4,000 pairs. Long, cold winters don't favour these 34cm-high birds, which find it hard to catch voles hidden under the snow. Once seen, the Barn Owl is never forgotten, thanks to its heart-shaped white face and soft, moth-like flight. The unearthly shrieks, cries and hisses of the bird account for its occult image, along with an association with churches and graveyards. The scientific name comes from the Greek *tuto*, meaning night owl, and the Latin word for 'white', so it literally means 'white night owl'. Barn Owls pair up only once in their short lives and often breed just once or twice, which is hardly conducive to rapid and sustained population growth. Eggs are laid mainly in spring, dependent on food availability, with at least three in a brood, each two days apart. The young are dependent on the parents for up to three months from the time of egg-laying. Both parents are involved in rearing the young – with young Barn Owls able to eat their own body weight every night. During the three-month breeding season, it has been estimated that a pair of Barn Owls will take more than 1,000 rodents.

Mostly it is a pale
face hovering in the afterdraught
of the spirit, making both ends meet
on a scream. It is the breath
of the churchyard, the forming
of white frost in a believer,
when he would pray; it is soft
feathers camouflaging a machine
(R S Thomas: Barn Owl)

TJB. "Recently, a lady client of mine from France was visiting the studio to discuss a future commission and, as we walked around the bungalow, this large painting in our dining room caught her attention. 'Ah,' she exclaimed, 'La Dame Blanche.' In France, apparently, the Barn Owl is known as 'The White Lady'. While typically romantic, the name seems less appropriate when the cock bird is being illustrated and discussed. We won't stoop to calling it 'The White Bloke'... The old stable window in this painting was part of some very neglected and dilapidated farm buildings not far from my studio. Currently, a huge refurbishment and reinstatement of some of these old listed agricultural buildings is taking place, but before the work began I asked the owners if I could record some of the old building details for posterity."

Little Owl *(overleaf)*

TJB. "Surprise, surprise, another large tree painting – and another owl! I photographed this old pollarded lime tree about ten years ago and made a promise to myself that it would feature one day as part of a large painting. As it turned out, it was nearly eight years before I finally got round to using the image. At risk of stating the obvious, the larger and more complex the painting the longer it takes to complete. This inevitably results in one or two logistical problems. The yearly painting schedule allows for only one of these large pieces to be undertaken and, because of the extensive time involved (anything up to three months), it is a considerable investment for any client. Tackling another comprehensive work is always a financial gamble, but these are the paintings that bring me the most satisfaction. I never find the nature of a complex work boring – in fact, quite the opposite. The only real problem is that I have to persuade Jill that I will not undertake another until I have sold the last one!"

Fieldfare *(Turdus pilaris)*

UK conservation status: red
Habitat: forest, woodland, towns
Diet: invertebrates and fruit (especially in winter)
Also known as: Winter Thrush

Fallen apples and falling snow often bring Fieldfares into the garden, sometimes in large groups as they search out food. These large, colourful members of the Thrush family, measuring 26cm and standing very upright, will hop purposefully across open ground. They are very sociable birds, spending the winter in flocks of anything from a dozen to several hundred. Hawthorn hedges with berries are a favourite feeding area, with windfalls providing a much-needed substitute when the branches are bare. Fieldfares begin to arrive in Britain from late September onwards, becoming more numerous as the winter progresses. Numbers have been falling, along with those of so many Thrushes, with an estimated winter population of just 680,000 birds.

TJB. "If any individual bird conjures up fond recollections of my early bird-watching days on our family farm, it is the Fieldfare. This beautiful member of the Thrush family has many associations for me, one of which is that it usually signified the end of harvest, as the birds present themselves en-masse towards the end of September. The arrival of this northern visitor also coincided with the return to school after the summer holiday. However, for a few weeks, the evenings remained light enough for me to walk the fields and hedges with a cheap pair of borrowed binoculars hanging around my neck. Just watching and listening to these birds as they chattered and fed on the hedgerow berries is something that remains in my memory. Most people will, of course, look forward to the arrival of the spring migrants as they herald the warmer and longer days to come. The Fieldfare unfortunately does just the opposite, as the arrival of the bird and its cousin the Redwing is a portent of shorter days and lower temperatures. What fantastic winter guests they are. Given that Fieldfares are roughly the same size as our resident Mistle Thrush, they are quite capable of sorting out any of the more aggressive Blackbirds that try to compete for the limited food supply as winter progresses. My painting here shows a single cock Fieldfare taking advantage of the autumn crop of apples, a favourite food of all Thrushes. A few old eaters and cookers thrown out during the cold weather will guarantee a visit from this handsome bird. I am writing these notes during the last week of March and currently enjoying the sight of hundreds of Fieldfares and Redwings feeding on the local meadows and pasture prior to their return trip across the North Sea to the Scandinavian countries. I am always slightly sad to see them leave but, of course, any time now the Swallows and the rest of our summer visitors will be arriving."

Nuthatch

TJB. "Elsewhere in this book I have made reference to the number of illustrations and photographs of the Nuthatch that depict the bird in a head-down attitude. I am as guilty as anyone of this heinous crime. If I remember correctly, this is the only painting in which I have illustrated the Nuthatch moving on a tree in the opposite direction. The bird will, of course, feed in all manner of positions and, as a true arboreal species, it is capable of performing any number of acrobatic manoeuvres in order to seek out food hidden in the crevices of tree bark. This dead hawthorn branch caught my attention one sunny morning during a photographic walk through one of our local woods. It was the vivid ginger colour of the underside of the stripped bark that appealed. The colour resonated and worked well with the plumage of the Nuthatch, and I have to admit that I really did enjoy painting the bird heading 'north' for a change."

Chaffinch

TJB. "Had the House Sparrow been blessed with the striking plumage of the cock Chaffinch, I wonder if we would have been more kindly disposed towards it, instead of viewing it as a pest. It is strange to think that the Chaffinch is now the more widespread of the two species. This handsome resident Finch has always been a favourite of mine. It was the first widespread small bird that I came to know well and study with real interest. Numbers of Chaffinches have decreased slightly in recent years but, fortunately, the birds are still plentiful and now out-number Sparrows by a wide margin. Another thing that has changed since my early farm days is the colour of the string shown in the painting! Plastic baler twine arrived in the 1960s and replaced the old hemp-based string. As well as allowing artists to include an extra splash of colour in a composition, the material is virtually indestructible – and will probably outlast the gate depicted. When commissioned to paint a picture, clients sometimes enquire as to whether the quoted price includes the frame. I assure them that it is supplied as a complete item, including the picture cord and screws. In this particular work the customer will receive an additional piece of string at no extra cost!"

Teal (*Anas crecca*)

UK conservation status: amber
Habitat: lakes, marshes, ponds
and shallow streams
Diet: omnivorous, feeds mostly at
night in shallow water

The collective noun for this small
(36cm long), striking dabbling duck is a
'Spring', reflecting its near-vertical take-
off when disturbed. Winter numbers
can reach 200,000, but the summer
population is nearer 1,400 pairs.
The male wears a chestnut-coloured
hairpiece, sports broad-green eye
patches and boasts a yellow tail edged
in black. Found throughout Britain in
shallow waters, particularly important
winter locations include the Somerset
Levels and the Mersey Estuary.

TJB. "This is one of our smallest resident
ducks and, in my humble opinion, one
of the most attractive – particularly
the drake. All female ducks have a
less flamboyant colouration in order
to remain invisible during nesting, a
characteristic similar to that of most
game birds. During my 40-odd years as
a bird artist, I can recall painting only
four species of wildfowl: Mallard, Pintail,
Tufted Duck and this little fellow. All
wildfowl are superb aviators, but the
Teal is in a league of its own, quite simply
an aerobatic show-off. Small flocks of
Teal will perform fantastic aerobatics
seemingly just for enjoyment or exercise.
The funny thing about ducks is that
wildfowl enthusiasts often collect many
representatives of the genus from all
over the world. Ducks are their passion
and, generally, their ornithological
interest is reserved exclusively for
wildfowl. The only comparison I can
make is the obsession shown by
those with an interest in birds of prey,
particularly owls. Collectors will often
have substantial numbers of birds from
different parts of the globe, but show
little interest in birds in general. Mind
you, as regards the raptors and owls, I
really cannot blame them – they are a
fantastic group of birds."

Grey Wagtail

TJB. "The River Box runs through our neighbouring village (the name Boxford must relate to the period when there was no bridge in the main street), and Grey Wagtails nest regularly under the stonework of the bridge. The painting on the right was, however, completed as a result of inspiration gained during a visit to one of my favourite parts of North Wales: the RSPB reserve at Ynys-hir. Access to the hotel where Jill and I often stay necessitates crossing a small river, and these lovely birds are in evidence most days."

Ringed Plover *(Charadrius hiaticula)*

UK conservation status: amber
Habitat: sandy areas with low vegetation, estuaries
Diet: invertebrates; in winter, mostly marine worms and molluscs

Many British beaches in the summer will provide a glimpse of this attractive wader, but it blends in well with sand and shingle so is best spotted on the move. The Ringed Plover is a small (19cm long) and dumpy bird with short legs. It is brownish-grey above and almost white below, sporting an orange bill tipped with black. The legs are also orange, and the most obvious physical feature is the black-and-white pattern on its head and breast. In flight, the bird shows a broad white wing-stripe. While they generally breed on beaches, Ringed Plovers now also nest inland in sand and gravel pits. There are UK residents, but European visitors winter in Britain and birds from Greenland and Canada pass through on migration. The UK summer population is around 8,500 pairs.

TJB. "Birdwatchers and bird artists fortunate enough to live in East Anglia are blessed with a multitude of coastal reserves and natural habitats where they can study and enjoy a vast selection of waders and shore birds. However, being raised as a fledgling some distance from the coast, most of my experiences associated with wildlife were centred on or around the family farm. No doubt this is one of the reasons why a day trip or a holiday away from my own *habitat familiar* is always inspirational. I love exploring old fishing harbours and man-made derelict areas that are being reclaimed slowly by the natural world. Once again, with this particular painting, we are on the Suffolk coast. I am not too sure of the exact purpose of these small groins, but the colours and intricate combination of shapes of these redundant posts intrigued me sufficiently to attempt this large and complex work. As is often the case with my larger productions, the main character, in this case a Ringed Plover, is used simply as a raison d'etre in order to allow me to paint the surrounding location. Of course, any painting needs a subject and, as attractive as the setting was, it still needed a bird somewhere on the painting. This lovely little Plover is (another) of my favourites. I am not sure exactly how many stones I have featured in this composition, but there must be several hundred. I did try counting, but the telephone rang and I had to give up! What I can say for certain is that the pre-drawing took five days to complete and I enjoyed every minute of the process. I will leave it to the viewer of this work to make up their mind as to the scenario depicted here: is the bird simply resting, contemplating a nesting site or just sunbathing? Either way, it is not important; the finished work proved to be one of my most satisfying to undertake, but I will probably wait a few weeks before starting another picture featuring stones!"

Tree Sparrow

TJB. "On viewing this particular painting, I wonder if somebody will say, 'I thought that Tree Sparrows were woodland birds'. Well, yes, they do have an association with trees – or, to be strictly accurate, they nest in trees and will utilise old Woodpecker holes or similar openings. However, the species is really a farmland bird, very rarely taking up residence in a suburban environment. Like its close cousin the House Sparrow, the Tree Sparrow is predominantly a grain and seed-eater, but small invertebrates and the odd scrap of vegetation will form part of the bird's 'five a day'! It is, of course, the reliance on this seed-based diet that has contributed significantly to the downturn in fortunes of this handsome little bird. Modern agricultural practices and the farming calendar now make it very difficult for the Tree Sparrow to maintain its former numbers, particularly during the winter. I can recall as a youngster on our Suffolk farm taking for granted the flocks that would feed on over-wintering stubble; I haven't seen one on my own patch for years. A few months ago, Jill and I were visiting a client and friend in Lincoln and on the way home to Suffolk we stopped overnight at Rutland Water, a favourite spot of ours. As is my habit, I took an early-morning walk along the shore of the reservoir before breakfast and, while standing watching the mist lift off the water, I became aware of a familiar sound. I was struggling to place this particular little ditty until I noticed several little brown jobs bouncing about in the hedge opposite. A quick check with the binoculars and there they were – Tree Sparrows, lots of them! Presumably, the mixed arable and livestock farm that bordered this part of the water provides the birds with everything they need on a daily basis – it certainly made my day."

Goldfinch
(Carduelis carduelis)

UK conservation status: green
Habitat: woodland, farmland,
open country, gardens
Diet: small seeds; some
invertebrates in summer
Also known as: Redhead

While the collective noun 'charm' applies to all finches, most people would agree that it is particularly appropriate for this highly coloured bird with a bright-red face and yellow wing patch. Squabbling groups can be lured into gardens with nyjer seed feeders, although they look still more charming when flocking around wild thistles and teasel heads. Goldfinches often breed in loose colonies, and have a liquid, twittering song. In winter, many UK birds migrate as far south as Spain. The UK population of this little (12cm-long) charmer occupies an estimated 300,000 territories.

TJB. "Whenever I am asked to paint this lovely little finch, the client usually requests that the setting should include thistles. Who am I to argue? However, thistle heads are available only for a few months of the year, and many other types of seeds are therefore consumed. Teasels are another end-of-season food source, along with many of the seed heads of the compositae family of plants (including bettany and groundsel). An intriguing fact relating to the difference between the sexes of Goldfinches is that the cock bird possesses a slightly longer bill. This means that it can poke further into some of the seed heads than the female – teasel in particular. The provision of nyjer seeds in gardens has resulted in this normally very rural species visiting in large numbers. I have two substantial feeders in place that require filling every two days."

Robin

TJB. "Yes, I know, 'Robin on a tap' – not that original! I suspect that there are countless images, paintings and photographs showing this ever-popular garden bird perched on a tap or a fork handle. Earlier in this book (page 29) you can find one of mine lurking among the flower pots. In my defence, I have always resisted the temptation to illustrate the bird sitting in a holly bush covered in snow! However, if my memory serves me well, this is only the second time I have depicted such an overtly familiar scene. The real reason was that I wanted to paint this particular old farm tap (that's my excuse, and I'm sticking to it!). Elsewhere in this book I mention how birds will often seek out any object poking above the surrounding vegetation, seemingly finding these vantage points irresistible. Taps, gates, garden tools and posts will be used time and again as observation points. In this instance, both the Robin and I have taken a fancy to the same old tap."

Grey Wagtail

TJB. "Elsewhere in this book I have mentioned that I will occasionally incorporate a particular item to strengthen and form the basis of a composition. This old chain, lying in the mud at Southwold Harbour, appealed enormously and I therefore photographed it from several angles. The same small section of discarded chain formed the secondary subject in a previous painting of a Pied Wagtail. This work, showing a Grey Wagtail, was intended to form part of a planned trio – a group of paintings depicting all three Wagtails that are on the British list. However, the Pied Wagtail was sold within a few days of completion and, as it turned out, this Grey Wagtail ended up as a larger and different format painting. So much for careful planning! As you will have gathered from the contents of this book, the Wagtails are a favourite subject of mine. The shape and colouring of the birds simply lend themselves to illustration. Strictly speaking, the Grey Wagtail is a bird that is generally associated with running water. Streams and rivers are the preferred habitat, and my recollections of the species are always associated with photographic trips to Wales and the West Country, with their wonderful natural landscapes. However, in this instance, long-distance travel from the studio is not a prerequisite – we have a pair of Grey Wagtails nesting under the bridge in my local village."

Wheatear *(Oenanthe oenanthe)*

UK conservation status: amber
Habitat: open country
Diet: mostly insects, other invertebrates, berries

There is an impolite 'common' name for the Wheatear, which describes in crude terms its pale posterior! Such indignities aside, this charming 15cm-long bird is a summer-visiting ground dweller, often seen perched on moorland rocks looking for insects. Blue/grey in colour, it has an orange flush on the breast, and shows its infamous white rump when in flight. Wheatears breed mainly in western and northern Britain and western Ireland, with the British summer population exceeding half-a-million. They winter in central Africa.

TJB. "Earlier this year, in April to be precise, Jill and I, with a couple of friends, drove to Devon to deliver a painting to a client who lived on the edge of Dartmoor. Grabbing the opportunity to combine business with pleasure, we decided to take a short break and stay on the Devon/Cornwall border. Business complete, I suggested to Ralph (designated driver for the trip) that, as we had plenty of time before our planned arrival at our hotel, we should leave the motorway and drive across Dartmoor. While we were enjoying a delicious cream tea in a delightful restaurant garden, I explained to the assembled company that a casual excursion across the moor would reward us with sightings of some special birds: Wheatears, Ring Ouzels, Buzzards and possibly a Merlin. Clutching binoculars in eager anticipation, we began our journey across the centre of the moor. An hour or so later we arrived at our hotel, having seen nothing at all – not even a Wheatear. I have no idea why. Perhaps we were just unlucky. Normally Dartmoor is alive with these little chaps. No doubt they were watching us trying to watch them! A few years ago, holidaying in North Wales, Jill and I had a little more luck. Not only were Wheatears, Stonechats and Pipits everywhere, but this particular cock bird was hawking out over the water after insects at a roadside lake. We sat in the comfort of the car watching the bird going about its daily business. This painting was the result."

Goshawk *(Accipiter gentilis – previous page)*

UK conservation status: green
Habitat: forest, open woodland
Diet: birds and mammals up to the size of brown hare; high-speed pursuit over short distances
Also known as: Pigeon Hawk

Rare, but not considered endangered, the Goshawk is a truly memorable raptor of almost Buzzard-like proportions, but wearing a much sharper outfit. Males are typically around 20 per cent smaller than female birds and are dressed in blue-grey above with horizontal grey stripes below. Females, which grow to 55cm in length and have a wingspan of 150cm, are brownish-grey on top, with brown stripes underneath. The Goshawk has a look that can almost kill on its own, sporting a fierce stare from bright-red eyes topped by distinctive white eyebrows. It can hunt at high speed, thanks to broad wings. In common with the much smaller Sparrowhawk, it will weave at speed in and out of trees, showing great agility for such a large bird. Goshawks are still persecuted by man, and their nests continue to be robbed. In spite of this, the population appears to be growing slowly, with mature conifer plantations providing a good home in Wales and Scotland. Recent statistics suggest there are approximately 400 pairs in the UK.

TJB. "Until you have got up close and personal with one of these magnificent hawks, it is impossible to describe the sheer beauty and personality of the bird. Goshawks can be as big as Buzzards but, at that point, the similarity ends. Buzzards are almost benign in temperament, their flight is often languid and lazy, and the bird exhibits a friendlier demeanour. None of these characteristics applies to the Goshawk. The large painting in this book was undertaken over a period of many weeks following a visit to a falconer and breeder of these stunning raptors. The lady in my painting is based on a large five-year-old female named Angelique. I spent a very interesting hour or so locked in the aviary with this lovely hawk and, while I was studying and photographing her, she would sit obligingly, taking a great interest, in turn, in my photographic equipment and in me. This is a true hawk, a member of the *Accipiter* family, a classification that includes our only other resident member of the genus, the Sparrowhawk (another favourite subject of mine). There is no excuse for confusing a Goshawk with a Sparrowhawk. Cock Sparrowhawks are smaller than the female, and the cock Goshawk is far bigger than the hen Sparrowhawk. As the female Goshawk is bigger still, there is really no comparison. A hen bird can weigh almost 3lb, against 10oz for a female Sparrowhawk – less than a quarter of the weight of the larger raptor. The dramatic difference in size exhibited by the two sexes among such birds is referred to as reversed-size sexual dimorphism. I have been lucky enough to observe Goshawks soaring over conifer plantations in North Wales but, alas, have never encountered the bird in a full-on pursuit of prey. What an exciting sight that must be for the spectator, as the ghostly apparition weaves around the tree trunks. Woe betide the squirrel or Wood Pigeon that does not see it coming."

Acknowledgements

TJB, Kersey, July 2011:

This, from the artist's point of view, has to be one of the most important pages in the book. Why? Simply because the people I am about to thank are the ones who were responsible for making the whole project possible. You may be one of those people who skips past the Acknowledgements page with a promise to read it later. Even worse, you may be someone who doesn't read it at all. Whatever the case, you should be ashamed of yourself and must seek penance from the artist by purchasing another six copies of this book!

Seriously, though, it really is a far more complicated and time-consuming process to produce a volume such as this than most people would imagine. My authors and editors, Alan and Marion, took on the demanding task of designing and laying out the book: their experience and expertise resulted in a finished work that far exceeded my expectations. Alan's informative and entertaining text has complemented my small narrative contributions (known fondly as 'scribbles'), while the pair of them fine-tuned my picture-related ramblings. I may be lucky enough to be described as a reasonably gifted bird artist, but when it comes to the written word (especially the long ones) I am truly grateful for their professional input.

Andrew and Graham of the Wildlife Art Gallery in Lavenham must also step into the spotlight and take a bow, having been the original perpetrators of the book. The idea grew like topsy from their original suggestion that we celebrate my 65th birthday exhibition by producing a slightly 'upmarket' catalogue for the show. This wonderful book is the result.

Last, but certainly not least, a huge debt of gratitude goes to my wife, Jill. Not only did she transfer my illegible scribbles from sketchpad to screen but, ever since our first meeting in 1966, she has supported and encouraged me in my risky career. Many would consider wildlife art to be a shaky foundation on which to build a loving and long-lasting relationship. Sweetheart, you are my secretary, business manager, domestic goddess and pillar of strength that has propped me up for the last 47 years. Without your support, I would have collapsed long ago!

ADMM, Sutton, July 2011:

Thanks go to my wife, business partner and chief sub-editor Marion. Her input to the book was invaluable and her daily support priceless. Keep well — we've got so much more to look forward to.

Thanks to Terry and Jill for allowing us to be involved in the project and for tolerating the invasion of your home and busy lives. We would like to help you with the 70th birthday book, so keep painting!

Graham and Andrew at the Wildlife Art Gallery were enthusiastic and supportive throughout the process. Thanks for introducing us to wildlife art — we owe you a lot, but you possibly owe us more!

To my folks down in Sussex, I hope you enjoy Terry's pictures and my words. Hopefully this won't be the last book with my name on it.

Finally, farewell to Plum, our 20-year-old Indian Ringneck Parakeet, who shuffled off her perch during the production of this book. Perhaps Terry will one day paint a bird just like you...

The big pond at Little Paddock. Overleaf: Kestrel and Nuthatch.

Kestrel

TJB. "Here is an interesting fact and one that is possibly well-known to anyone who specialises in photographing birds in their garden. Stick a post in the ground in a suitable area, and within minutes I guarantee that something will come and sit on it – probably a Robin or any one of the resident common garden species. I am sure that most people would be amazed at how readily birds perch on top of a post or a stick – or any other protruding item, for that matter. Some locations, such as field gate posts, electricity poles or dead trees, will be adopted by the local avian population as regular and vital vantage points from which they will sing, hunt or just generally pass the time of day. Why am I mentioning this? Well, people viewing a painting occasionally remark, 'Haven't you used that post before?'. The answer is, 'Yes, probably'. Nothing wrong with that, particularly if the post or gate in question is attractive and challenging to paint. If so, I will incorporate it in different pictures over a period of years. This old meadow gate has served just such a purpose for several paintings and, apart from the addition of old wire or binder twine depending on my mood, it remains recognisable in two or three previous works. This particular gate was located in a neighbour's meadow, and a few weeks ago I wandered over to reacquaint myself. Sadly, it is now just a photographic memory. In its place hangs a brand-new galvanised steel arrangement. Undoubtedly it will last a lifetime and serve its purpose admirably, but I doubt this new gate will ever provide the inspiration for a painting!"

Index of paintings

Work in progress: Kestrel perched on a wood pile located not far from Terry's studio at Little Paddock. Virtually everything that is to appear in Terry's finished painting will be drawn painstakingly in pencil on to the prepared board.